Sunset
Children's
Rooms
& Play Yards

By the Editors of Sunset Books
and Sunset Magazine

Lane Publishing Co., Menlo Park, California

We gratefully acknowledge...

...the following individuals and companies for their encouragement and assistance in gathering the material for this book: Jeanne Clark, Gene Clements, The Cotton Works, Roy Davis, Gymnastics West, Sharon Owen Haven, House of Today, Kiyoko Ishimoto, Karen Loy, Tina Meyers, Minimal Space, Poppy Fabrics, Linda J. Selden, Anne Stewart, Antonio Torrice, and Joanne Woods. And a special thank-you goes to the designers whose names appear throughout the book.

Supervising Editor:
Susan Warton

Staff Editors:
Kathryn L. Arthurs
Barbara G. Gibson

Special Consultants:
Peter O. Whiteley
Assistant Editor, Sunset Magazine
Diana Bunce
Staff Editor, Sunset Magazine

Design:
Timothy Bachman
JoAnn Masaoka Lewis

Artwork:
Sandra E. Popovich

Cover:
Circus-bright fabrics cover playful foam sculptures designed by Patricia Moser. You'll see their full potential on pages 44 and 45. The room on the cover was designed by James Caldwell and photographed by Darrow M. Watt.

Photographers

Richard Fish: 19 bottom left, 91 bottom, 94 top. **Frank Jensen:** 11 top. **Steve W. Marley:** 3, 11 bottom, 19 bottom right, 27 right, 28 top, 29 left, 54 top, 70 top left and right. **Ells Marugg:** 54 bottom right. **Don Normark:** 19 top, 30 bottom. **Norman A. Plate:** 22 bottom, 94 bottom. **Bill Ross:** 13 bottom. **Darrow M. Watt:** 4, 5, 6, 12, 13 top left and right, 14 20, 21, 22 top left and right, 27 top left and bottom left, 28 bottom, 29 right, 30 top and center, 35, 36, 37, 38, 43, 44, 45, 46, 51, 52, 53, 54 bottom left, 59, 60, 61, 62, 67, 68, 69, 70 bottom, 75, 76, 77, 78, 83, 84, 85, 86, 91 top left and right, 92, 93.

Editor, Sunset Books: David E. Clark

Sixth printing August 1985

Contents

Children's Rooms 4-67

Sand frigate sails the high, leafy seas (see also page 70).

Play Yards 68-95

Index 96

Children's Rooms

Children's bedrooms mean so much more to them than places to sleep (usually the least popular use) that the physical space involved begs for a better name..."nursery" for the very young, or "lair" for boisterous types, or maybe "habitat" for just about any child.

So much goes on in this one corner of the world that is unquestionably a child's very own. In happiest circumstances, the surroundings serve as living room, kitchen, library, music room, budding artist's studio, mad scientist's lab — not to mention intergalactic space ship or junior discotheque.

No matter what we call them, the chunks of real estate that we allot to our offspring are hard-working and mercurial spaces. To design them wisely and ruggedly demands a fair amount of ingenuity, allowing for needs that will change from hour to hour as well as from year to year.

Naturally, we want to create a friendly, cozy, and safe environment — and, at the same time, we hope it will stay fairly shipshape over the years. Because kids' rooms are often undersized, compared to the clutter they must absorb, the furnishings we choose and the way we arrange them make a big difference.

If all of that sounds daunting enough to boggle a parent's brains, take heart. As you will see in this chapter, many families have come up with diverse and imaginative solutions to typical children's room problems. You'll notice that many different routes were taken to solve the problems, but all led to exciting results.

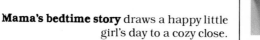

Mama's bedtime story draws a happy little girl's day to a cozy close.

If Baby so much as hiccups, the *angilhisaun* cradle bobs and sways gently on its ceiling-anchored spring. Directions for building this Eskimo cradle—which is transportable from living room to nursery to back garden —appear on page 8. Design adaptation: Douglas Stewart.

Baby gazes with wonder at his image (and Mama's, too) in the looking glass. His changing table sits inside an opened-up closet. Architect: James Caldwell.

Little "Moses in the bulrushes" takes the air on a summer afternoon, lying snug in a large, go-everywhere basket. (Next year, it can carry a picnic or firewood.)

Just a few nursery notions...

Ah, the bonny wee babe with its fist tightly clutching its blanket. In the first weeks at home, it may sleep most comfortably and conveniently in its parents' bedroom.

The requirements of a first nursery are simple: all you need are a cozy bed, a comfortable spot for feeding, a changing surface that is easy on your back, and plenty of fresh air and visual cheer.

Baby's bed

During your baby's first weeks, a bureau drawer or large wicker basket, equipped with a firm mattress and padded sides, makes an excellent, snug bed. As your baby grows, of course you'll need something bigger, like a crib.

Today's crib was originally designed in the late 19th century, when doctors feared that rocking a baby in a cradle might spoil it and might even foster brain damage. Cribs are still popular as an economical and practical first bed. But if you choose one, keep in mind that it makes an enormous bed for a newborn. Make it a smaller nest by filling one end in with firm cushions (the ticking of a wind-up clock tucked among them sometimes soothes babies just as it does puppies).

Despite the Victorians' qualms, there is really much to be said for the age-old cradle with its gently pacifying motion. A suspended version (such as the Alaskan baby bed shown on the facing page) can be moved from one room to another, or even outdoors—wherever you have a strong, safely secured hook for it (see "Anchor it safely," page 57). Directions for the cradle appear on the next page.

You might want to invest in a baby buggy, either new or previously occupied, to serve as a bed. Besides strolling with it in the park, you can wheel this lovely vehicle throughout the house, giving it a lulling jiggle if Baby whimpers as you cook or water the fern.

Serenity

For feeding and relaxing with your new son or daughter, provide yourself a comfortable place to sit or recline. Most mothers and babies love rocking chairs—but you may prefer a mattress with plenty of pillows, or even a wide hammock.

For Baby's sake (as well as your own, during night feedings), keep artificial lighting soft.

Visual stimulation

Very early, your baby will enjoy good things to look at. Bright colors and movement attract and delight the infant eye. They also create a mood of welcoming cheer in the nursery.

You might want to stitch a soft sculpture mobile like the one shown above. When Baby pulls on the ribbons, the satin "pillows" bounce on elastic cord.

Let your eye roam also to other sources of visual cheer: colorful cloth or paper kites to hang from the ceiling; a bit of stained glass or strips of bright featherweight cloth, hung to catch sunlight in the window; paper parasols, lanterns, or accordion-folded party decorations; even a few choice Christmas trimmings. Also, a bowl of swishing goldfish makes a baby coo with delight.

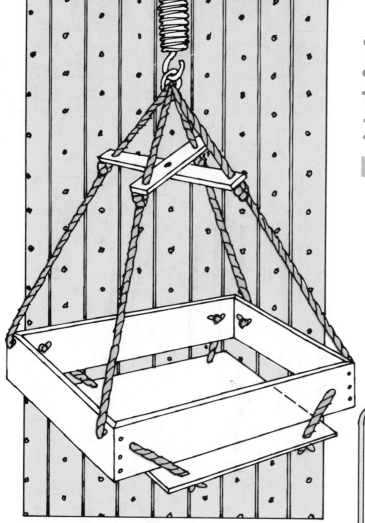

Eskimo cradle

You can hang the cradle shown on page 6 from a ceiling beam indoors or from a tree limb outside (to read how to anchor its hook securely, see page 57). Construction is quite simple.

You need four 1 by 4s (two 24 inches long, two 36 inches long), a 20 by 24-inch sheet of 1/4-inch tempered hardboard, two 18-inch-long 1 by 2s, and some 3/8-inch-diameter nylon rope (on the cradle we show, the rope is covered with decorative macramé). A 1-inch-diameter spring (garage-door type) can be added so that the bed will jiggle as the baby moves.

Glue and nail the 1 by 4s together to make the frame; bolt the 1 by 2s together in the middle to form a spreader, as shown in the drawing. Drill 7/16-inch holes for the rope in the corners of the hardboard, frame, and spreader, and assemble as shown above by knotting and threading the rope. Suspend the hardboard a few inches below the frame. For extra coziness, lap a small quilt over cradle sides and floor, stapling it underneath. Then lay bedding on top.

Garden-style safety gate

When shopping for a toddler's restraining gate, little Monique's parents felt that most of what they saw was unsightly, if not downright dangerous. Here's the alternative they designed to keep their daughter out of harm's way. It's charming enough that, even though Monique no longer needs it for her safety, she still loves to play with it.

The gate is built of 1 3/8-inch lattice glued to a square frame of 1 by 2s. It is hinged to the outside of the door jamb, and closes with a sliding lock on the outside.

Dresser-top changing table

By adding temporary roll bars to the top of a roomy chest of drawers, you can create a changing table that will continue its service through the years.

Matthew's father went one step further: he jigsawed a decorative top edge along the back roll bar. His son likes to trace its pastoral silhouettes with his hands while undergoing a diaper change.

The decorative back bar is made from ³/₄-inch plywood; the sides are cut from 1 by 4-inch pine. Matthew's father cut the back bar following a pattern sketched on a long strip of paper. The sides were simply rounded down at the front to meet the top of an unfinished wood dresser. After careful sanding, the side bars were attached to the back bar with woodscrews and glue. Where the back bar joins the dresser, corner braces and screws are placed out of sight at the back. The sides fasten to the top of the dresser with two vertically countersunk screws near the front.

For preschool Picassos

Here is a low but expansive paper-dispensing table, designed by the mother of two young artists. Its surface is a 28 by 80-inch hollow-core door; supports and legs are clear fir. A large roll of paper (check with a newspaper plant or butcher supplier) revolves on a dowel at one end; plastic dish tubs, mounted on runners, slide out from underneath the table, like drawers.

Buy the paper roll first, then choose a dowel that will fit its opening and allow the roll to revolve freely. Positioning of the dowel on its upright supports will depend on the thickness of the paper roll.

Buy the plastic dish tubs before attaching the legs. Calculate the spacing of the legs by measuring the width of a tub just below its lip and adding the width of the runners on which the tub will slide.

Fasten all pieces with white glue and woodscrews, except for the dowel (which must be removeable from the holes in its supports). Sand and apply the finish of your choice.

Kitchen step-up box

Three-year-old William can carry his hollow cube from its low cupboard to the sink, to get a drink of water, or to the kitchen counter when he wants to help the cook (but only when his parents wish: the cupboard has a safety catch). Made from 5 feet of 1 by 10-inch pine, glued and nailed together with 2-inch finishing nails, the cube is wide enough for steady standing. For reinforcement, chamfer strips are glued to the inside corners. As an extra precaution, in case of a little spilled water, William's father added safety treads.

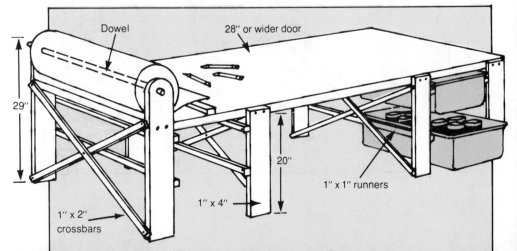

Dowel — 28" or wider door — 29" — 20" — 1" x 1" runners — 1" x 4" — 1" x 2" crossbars

Indoor romps for tiny Tarzans

Not long after a toddler's first steps comes every parent's favorite phase of childhood —the big Energy Explosion. This is the era in which most kids find it nearly impossible to slow down to a walk. Their seemingly constant motion —running, jumping, climbing, tumbling, wriggling —can be fun for everyone, but exhausting, too.

How can a run-ragged parent channel such boundless energy, especially when weather conditions keep everyone cloistered indoors? One way is to provide your small whirlwind with one of the good commercial indoor swings or kiddie gyms available today (for safety tips on hanging such play equipment, see page 57). Some further energy-dispensing ideas are shown here.

A new look at ladders

For children more than 3 or 4 years old, straight, wooden, round-runged ladders (such as you would find at a hardware store) provide all kinds of valuable coordination-improving experiences. More important: They're fun for your small monkeys to clamber on.

Try hanging a 6-foot ladder horizontally from the ceiling (see "Anchor it safely," page 57), using four heavy screw eyes and four doubled lengths of lightweight (but strong) chain. Position it so that it won't crash into the wall when swinging forward or back, or from side to side. The position of each screw eye should correspond to a corner of the ladder. Thread a chain through one screw eye. Slide one end of the chain under the corresponding end of the ladder's side; loop it back over the outermost rung and under the side. Connect the two chain ends with a padlock, adjusting length as necessary to give the ladder the right height. Repeat with the other three chains. Hang the ladder just out of reach —about 10 or 12 inches above your child's head height —so that Tarzan or Jane will have to take a little leap to catch one of the rungs.

On days when everyone is ready to climb the walls, why not let them do it? Bolt a ladder vertically to the wall studs —and suddenly you have an indoor mini-gym that takes practically no space at all.

First, measure the distance between your wall studs (usually about 14 inches; to locate the studs, consult page 57). You will need three crosspieces of 2 by 4 lumber, each long enough to extend over three wall studs. Drill each crosspiece in three places, to correspond to the spacing of the studs.

Next, center the ladder against the crosspieces and screw the ladder's sides securely to the crosspieces. Finally, screw the crosspieces tightly to the wall studs, through the previously drilled holes. In each case, use wood screws or lag bolts long enough to penetrate at least 2 inches.

Fold-up maze

This toy becomes, by turns, a labyrinth to explore, a playhouse, or just a freeform building toy.

To construct it, start with one or more 4 by 8-foot sheets of styrene foam board, sold at art supply stores. With a utility knife, slice the sheet into rectangles or into squares measuring 2 feet or larger (one 4 by 8-foot sheet can be cut into eight 2-foot squares). Cut large holes in some of the squares to make entrances and exits. Reinforce edges with wide masking tape, and with the same tape, join the squares on one side only, allowing them to hinge back on themselves. This way, they will fold up accordion-style. Let your kids paint them or cover them with contact paper (first "dust" the styrene foam with a cloth so the paint or paper will adhere).

Call it a "gymni-sleep." This cross between bunkbeds and a playground has everything that a boisterous little body could need on a cold, wet day: swing, slide, trapeze bar, and basketball net; innumerable places to climb; and a cozy mid-level pad for reading. You might want to add a sturdy ladder, and place thick carpeting underneath for extra safety. Design: Sheldon Smith.

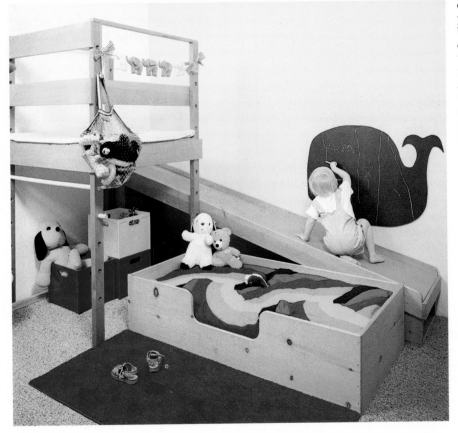

Neatly fitted to the scale of a city apartment, this sleeping-climbing-sliding-hiding play structure gives Gabriel all kinds of romping fun. His father built it when Gabriel outgrew his crib at age two. Extra climbing dowels will fit between the upright supports when he is a little older. Design: Donald W. Vandervort.

With traffic light excitement, two strong primary colors team up against a clean expanse of white. The more blazing red is kept in rein as a bright accent against the grass-green wall. Design: Karen Loy.

Color them a cheerful world

Sophisticated earth tones and tepid pastels may be favored by sophisticated adults. But children, as a rule, have a wider awake color sense: to them, often (but not always), the brighter it is, the better. As you decorate their rooms with paint, fabrics, carpeting, or all three, give them vivid, even loud colors. (Just take care not to go riotously overboard—too much color stimulus will overwhelm anyone.)

Of course, your child's age and personality will affect your color selection as well as other decorating considerations. Be sure you consult your son or daughter about preferences before you forge ahead. Go window shopping together. Bring home fabric swatches and paint sample cards for after-dinner selection games (such things make great materials for later art projects, too).

The chances are good that your own emotional responses to different colors will be similar to your children's, though they may favor a bolder and brighter personal environment. Grass green and sunny yellow generally evoke a fresh and cheerful feeling in people of all ages. Blue tends to pacify the spirit (used in excess, though, the deeper tones tend to be depressing). Children usually relish red (but, again, avoid an excess of this rousing color). And though primary colors are traditional favorites of the young, don't neglect to consider intermediates like orange or lavender, which can offer just as much warmth and good cheer. Any rainbow hue you choose will glow brightly against white.

Simple tricks with cotton prints lend cheer to a small boy's private world. Stretched fabric panels make up his picture gallery, and at naptime he likes to gaze at his "canopy"—simply a length of cloth draped from ceiling beams. Design: Patricia C. Woerner.

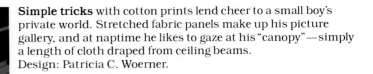

A palette of warm colors, splashed casually against pale surroundings, infuses this nursery with a fresh and airy spirit. Architect: James Caldwell.

Delicious as crayons to a child's eye are these primary-color walls, used to set a raised play platform apart from the more subdued sleeping portion of the bedroom. Architect: Ronald Quigley.

Squeezing every last inch out of a tight space, built-in cabinets and a folding desk make it possible to sleep as many as three children in this room. When the desk hinges out of the way (see detail), you can pull out a trundle bed. Cabinetry: Norman Shaw.

Storage cubes, stacked and bolted together, free extra play space in this 10 by 11-foot room, shared by two energetic boys. Both bunks are elevated on the stacked cubes, which were purchased from an unfinished-furniture store.

Kids need elbow space & knee room

Coping with skimpy space is one of the most common problems faced by parents as they plan a child's bedroom. For adults, who really need little more than a place to put the bed and a few square yards for getting dressed, the small-scale bedroom typical of recently built homes may be adequate. But children have innate tendencies—as well as special needs—that make space planning more complicated. For a number of early years, they like to spread out on the floor to play. Often, too, they have to share the bedroom with a sibling. Even if they don't share, they need extra furniture because their room is a diverse activity center, not just a place to sleep. And finally, most kids accumulate a lot of cumbersome possessions that they don't often keep neatly stored out of sight.

You'll find ideas for freeing floorspace sprinkled throughout this chapter. For your family's needs, bunkbeds might be the answer—a variety of designs appear on the next few pages. If clutter and ease of cleanup are a special problem, look through the storage ideas on pages 24 to 27.

Opposite this page are photographs of small bedrooms where ingenuity with built-in furniture yielded maximum sprawl-out space. And below is a description of a very novel arrangement that offers not only extra floorspace, when desired, but also adaptability to a child's changing needs.

A room on ropes

Borrowing its style from the circus, one of the most imaginative small-space solutions we found is a trapezelike bedroom rigged up with bright yellow nylon ropes. The 8 by 12-foot room contains inexpensive, simple-to-make, and lightweight furnishings—all suspended from the ceiling. Ropes (3/8 inch in diameter) support shelves, a swing, and—for bedtime stories—an adult's swivel chair with its legs removed. (For an older child, you could add larger gymnastic challenges—a trapeze bar or a rope ladder.)

More yellow rope, threaded through pulleys, rigs a diaper-changing shelf that pulls up and out of the way when not in use.

For safety, each article of furniture hangs from four ropes and sturdy hooks screwed into ceiling joists (to read how to locate joists and secure hooks, see page 57). Just below the hooks, metal thimbles—available from boat supply stores—protect the swing-seat ropes from the wear of friction.

Ceiling joist hooks were placed in a grid pattern, 16 inches apart. (An electric drill made the work go quickly.) This enables the shelves, rocking swivel chair, and swing to be moved from one area of the room to another.

Swing seat, shelves, and underneath support for the chair were cut from 1-inch lumber. Lengths of rope were pushed through holes drilled in the four corners of each piece and knotted underneath.

Set up a room with moving parts... Fold-downs, roll-outs, raise-ups & pull-outs

Roller-skating storage

There is a subtle but sure psychological advantage to a toy bin that rolls on casters — it's a lot more fun than one that doesn't. When cleanup time arrives, it becomes a truck to drive back into its garage (under a desk or counter, under the bed, or in the closet). While it's out rolling, it can travel to various rooms with various kinds of cargo. It may bump into walls occasionally, but you can glue a strip of padding around its rim.

Make a simple open cube of plywood or particle board (a building plan appears on page 49). Or use the triple-layer cardboard discussed on page 50. If you don't want to make it yourself, you can purchase cubes from an unfinished furniture dealer. If round shapes delight you, look for a heavy fiber drum (suppliers are listed in the Yellow Pages under "Barrels and Drums"). Attach four large casters of good quality to the base of whichever bin you choose. Place a block of wood in the bottom of the bin for each caster screw to penetrate. For stability, fix the casters as close to the outside corners as you can manage.

The Murphy solution

Made famous as an escape route by Charlie Chaplin and other early slapstick film stars, the Murphy bed either folds up or slides into a closet, instantly emptying a room of disorderly linens and at least 18 square feet of useless bulk.

Today, you might have to move the family into an old-time boarding house to find an authentic "In-a-dor" bed. But here is an up-to-date adaptation of William L. Murphy's marvelous invention.

Our "Murphy" might be more accurately described as a folding chalkboard. Pivoting down from the wall, it sleeps either Junior or an overnight guest. In its "up" position, it becomes a surface for artistic expression of generous proportions.

Its base and sides are built like a shallow box of $3/4$-inch plywood. The good face of the base plywood is placed down to form the bed's underside, and painted with chalkboard paint. A 1 by 1, fastened (either nailed and glued, or screwed) to the sides, supports the base, and plywood triangles at the bottom corners add strength. The frame can be designed to hold either a cot-sized or a standard mattress.

The bed — which is actually an upper bunk — pivots down on a 6-foot piano hinge, screwed to a hardwood strip anchored to wall studs. A heavy chain, securely fastened at one end to a wall stud or ceiling joist (see page 57) and, at the other, to an end corner of the bunk, holds the bed level when it is folded down. At the head of the bunk, a 1 by 2 is screwed to the wall studs, further supporting the bed's weight. A short length of rope (also affixed to a wall stud) wraps around a boat cleat to hold the bunk in its raised position.

Disappearing desks

Whether supporting homework, chemistry experiments, or a jigsaw puzzle, a well-proportioned desk top is a very useful thing—as long as it is being used. At other times, it tends to block off space, get bumped against, and attract a confusion of clutter, since it is such a convenient spot to put things.

On the other hand, a desk that disappears when you don't need it is all the more appreciated when you do.

One such desk appears in the upper photograph on page 14. The 3/4-inch birch-faced plywood top of this folding desk is attached to the cabinet behind it with hinges. The desk is supported by 2 by 2-inch legs that pivot on bolts through an apron made of 1 by 3s glued to the underside of the plywood top. Magnetic catches hold the desk closed when the legs are folded and the desk lowered.

Another disappearing desk, shown in the photograph on page 35, works like the slide-in breadboard commonly found in kitchens. Actually, it is a shallow, inverted drawer, surfaced on the top and sides with plastic laminate. Its front is a 1 by 3, and its sides and back are 1 by 2s. The sides and back are glued and nailed to the desk top, a piece of 1/2-inch plywood. To prevent it from tipping when extended, the desk slides into its cabinet base between 1 by 1 guides, which are glued to the inner sides of the cabinet. A stop fastened to the back prevents the desk from being pulled out too far.

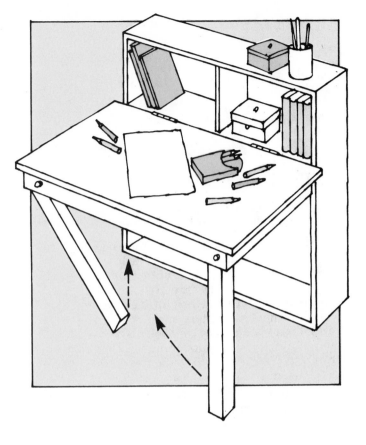

Elevating train board

A perennial Christmas favorite of many train-loving fathers (as well as quite a few sons and, doubtless, daughters too), a model railway takes up a lot of space after all of it has been set up. One father solves the problem by lifting the railway up to the ceiling when not in use.

Mounted on a heavy plywood board, the entire train layout is raised for storage, using a hand-cranked boat winch. Screws hold the winch to the studs of a wall corner so that the crank can turn freely. A single-wheel pulley and an eye bolt are attached within each corner of the board. Screw-in hooks hold four double-wheel pulleys to the ceiling beams.

Each of four ropes runs from the winch through one wheel of an overhead pulley, down through the corresponding board-mounted pulley, up through the second wheel of the ceiling pulley, then down again to attach to the eyebolt. The ropes can be removed, when desired, from the lowered board, which rests on sawhorses. Architect: Thomas Tomasi.

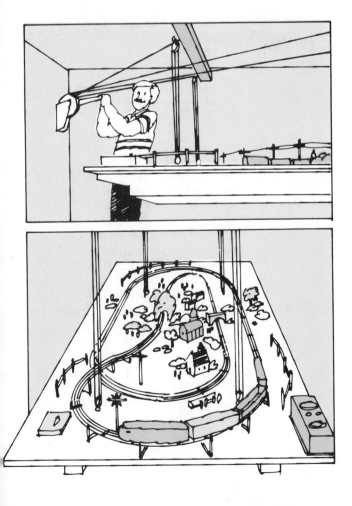

Sleeping high up... A favorite space-saver

For children and sailors, stacking beds have long been a solution to crowded sleeping quarters. As far as children are concerned, the system is generally sure to please. Forced by shortness of stature to look up at everyone except baby brothers and sisters, most children appreciate a spot from which they can look down at the world from time to time. An upper bunk, whether slept in by night or climbed into by day, provides just such a lofty—and relatively private—nook.

In planning, shopping for, or building bunks, safety should be your first consideration. You'll save yourself later anxiety, and possibly accidents as well.

The entire structure should be heavy and sturdy enough to accommodate several climbing kids at once. Make sure that the upper railing is strong, bearing in mind that children sometimes maneuver into odd locations during their sleep. Ladders or steps should be easily negotiable for the bunk owner (or owners). A base of wood slats, rather than wire, under the upper berth may prevent hair from becoming painfully caught in the "ceiling" of the lower bunk (check for adequate head-room, too). As a last precaution—in case someone does fall—try to provide thick carpeting around the base of the bunks.

While a stacking bed system abounds with virtues and remains a perennial favorite with kids, it sometimes does present problems. The worst, probably, is making the upper bed (especially for a not-very-agile parent). It helps to use a lightweight mattress, perhaps a slab of foam rubber, that you can lift off easily and cover with a fitted bottom sheet. Or you can sidestep the problem completely by giving your children washable sleeping bags that they can smooth down by themselves.

Another disadvantage to the upper bunk is likely to make itself felt if you live in a very warm climate or if the bedroom is poorly ventilated. In these conditions, sleeping on high sometimes becomes uncomfortable, because hot air rises to the ceiling.

Exploring new angles

Bunkbeds traditionally stack in two neat layers. However, if you are working out a design from scratch, you might survey other ways to orient the beds. Experiment with a floor plan of the bedroom and a paper card to simulate each bunk.

Create a right angle with the bunks in one corner, and you'll simultaneously create a little alcove-retreat or a nook where you can arrange desk and storage units. A right-angle plan also offers more head room for the occupant of the lower bunk.

Or, if you have a sufficiently long wall, put the bunks end-to-end. Each bed is quite separate this way (no more vexing kicks in the night for the upper occupant). And, again, you gain special play, work, or storage space under the elevated bed.

A very novel idea (shown in the lower right photograph on the facing page) is to raise both bunks. You may resolve a little rivalry at the same time.

From such a lofty vantage point, it's fun to look down on the world. And by raising the bed, you gain office space below. Design: Gerald Cichanski.

Headed for the kids-only zone, she climbs up to a comfortable corner retreat. Lacings of rope add to both safety and design of the raised bunks. Mural: Georgia LaRue. Bunk design: Tom Morrison.

These vinyl-sheathed cocoons — a bunk designer's response to the space age — are as cozy by night as they are sleek-looking by day. Design: Jim and Penny Hull.

Windows and portholes, for peeping through or puppetry, add to the appeal of these colorful sleep-and-play bunks. The lower one rests on purchased storage cubes eliminating the need for a separate bureau. Design: Sharon Owen Haven.

As if inspired by a Calder sculpture, the clean lines and clear colors of this bunk system immediately wake up the imagination—in both kids and adults. Design: Maynard Hale Lyndon.

Upstairs-downstairs sleep & play systems

Besides bedding you down at night, these bunks offer daytime tunneling, hiding, fish-watching, mountaineering, confiding in a friend, or setting up a store or puppet show—not to mention such prosaic activities as finishing homework or putting away toys.

With a few added shelves, spacious cupboards, and sliced-out windows, a basic bunk or loft structure becomes a friendly miniature world, promising endless variations on the freeform theme of play. Most of the ones shown here were owner-invented and not difficult to build. They incorporate ready-made units and shelves from an unfinished-furniture supplier. Sheets of hardboard or plywood, painted in smashing colors and sculpted with a jigsaw, add the final, fanciful touch.

Fantasia in marigold colors calls to mind a fairy tale castle. Extra surprises are the aquarium, tucked beside a cozy reading nook, and a long, L-shaped tunnel that runs under the desk and lower berth, all the way into the closet. Design: Sharon Owen Haven.

Like an elevator, a yellow pail hoists toys upstairs to the sleeping loft that is transformed —by turns — into a stage, a balcony, an airship, or simply a quiet spot for a game of cards.

High in their crow's-nest, two sisters share a moment of conviviality. Curtains shelter the lower bunk to make it a cozy retreat for reading—or a theater for puppets.

Bunkbed framing offers opportunities to add extra features: here, a clothes pole, affixed within children's reach, finishes off a handsome wood structure with a row of colorful dresses. Architect: John Schmid.

Of childproof solidity and functional design, these bunks also unbolt to become separate single beds. If the room were tall enough, even a third could be stacked on top. Architect: George Cody.

Bunkbed extras... Accessories for more fun

Bunkbed systems are usually massive and labyrinthine enough to make it easy to incorporate extra features. The upright and horizontal members of the basic structure form a sort of skeleton for accessories, whether the accessories are built in at the start or added later. Bunkbed systems can be varied almost infinitely, with a little imagination; here are a few suggestions.

Extra storage to go with bunks

As all parents discover early on, children are born pack rats. Every nook, cranny, bin, or shelf soon fills up with their personal effects —bizarre treasures, new and worn-out toys, oceans of books, papers, and puzzle pieces, not to mention clothing. For this reason, the most useful accessory you can add to your bunkbed system may be one or more extra places to put things.

In an L-shaped bunk system, you can place shelves and even a desk surface between the upright members that support the upper bed. If you make the shelves wide enough and use sturdy wood, they can even double as a ladder to the top.

An especially helpful extra in a room shared by siblings is lockable personal storage. A cabinet built into—or hung near—the headboard of each bunk (as shown in the photograph on the opposite page), and equipped with a lock, will be much appreciated by the occupants. Even if it doesn't lock, such a cabinet lends a sense of private territory to each bunk.

Cozy curtains

Even the simplest, most inexpensive cotton curtains will transform a lower bunk into a cozy private "cabin" for reading or playing house.

If you want to curtain your child's bunk, the simplest approach is to string fabric panels on tension rods that fit tautly between the bunk's upright supports, as shown in the photograph on the facing page. The whole apparatus slips out easily when you need to wash the curtains.

You may want to curtain all four sides, or just one, two, or three—it will probably depend on how many sides of the bed are open to the room. For the side where the child climbs in and out, make two fabric panels of equal size, so that, when hung, they will open at the center. Along the top of each panel, sew an open hem through which you can thread the rod; allow ample hem width—at least twice the thickness of the rod—this way, the curtains will push apart easily.

Interesting ups and downs

Getting up and down is more fun if you provide something to scale in addition to a ladder (always be sure to provide the ladder, too). For example, you might rig a heavy cotton climbing rope, secured to a ceiling joist close to the side of the upper berth; consult "Anchor it safely," on page 57.

One family built in a cabinet below the upper berth, with clothing drawers that double as climbing steps. It is important to make such drawers as deep and tight-fitting as possible, to prevent them from falling out when someone steps on them. Metal foot strips were fastened to the drawer openings for further safety. The face of each step was attached securely to the drawer side pieces with glue and wood screws, as shown below.

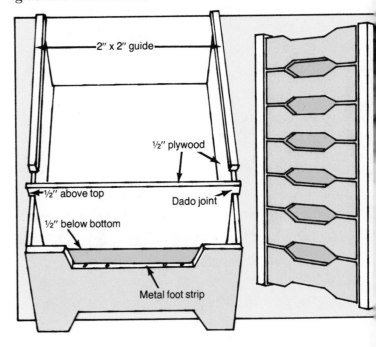

Order out of chaos...A place for everything

Preschooler's bedside table

The floor of this open cabinet slopes upward gently from back to front, preventing toys from tumbling out. A child can easily reach inside to take things out or put them away. Open to view, toys can be found at a glance. A roomy, tilted cabinet floor is an especially good idea for storing blocks, because they are so numerous and so inclined to topple.

Curiosity-seekers' containers

If you and your kids favor an eclectic look, shop around for storage containers that, in themselves, provoke curiosity and offer play potential. Here are a few suggestions: The hollow, revolving portion of a barber's pole (found by parents in a used office supply warehouse); a brightly painted old-fashioned metal breadbox; a good-size mailbox; a sturdy small suitcase or briefcase; a fishing tackle box with its myriad compartments; a carpenter's plastic carry-around toolbox. Older children with younger siblings appreciate boxes that they can lock.

Before using any previously occupied container, no matter how beautiful, check to make sure it's perfectly safe. Avoid anything with sharp edges, and steer clear of old, painted things, in case the paint contains lead. Finally, make sure your containers never held anything toxic or irritating.

Wall storage

Keeping lightweight toys, books, games, and other supplies on the wall frees extra floor space. For the very young, place shelves or other units within reach. An older child would probably enjoy a movable, safely locking ladder of the sort used in bookstores and libraries. Shelves with adjustable brackets allow flexibility as a child's size and needs change.

Painted or covered with wallpaper, circular containers cluster attractively on the wall in a colorful storage "collage." Large fiber drums (to find them, look in the Yellow Pages under "Barrels and Drums"), cut in slices, and with edges taped, make generous cabinets. Or at an art supply store, look for corrugated cardboard that you can roll into cylinders of various sizes; for sturdiness, allow two thicknesses for each cylinder, joining the layers with duct tape (a strong vinyl-backed tape available at hardware stores). Also tape on a cardboard base that you can nail to the wall for stability. Inexpensive but less rugged are heavy cardboard 3-gallon containers sold in some ice cream parlors.

Wooden fruit crates in sturdy and safe condition offer further alternatives. Wood soft drink boxes and — if you can find them — typesetters' drawers (castoffs from modernized printing plants) provide small compartments for miniatures and collections.

See-through organizers

When you can't find your purple crayon because it is hidden at the bottom of a coffee can, the usual solution is to dump the entire contents on the rug. But see-through storage alleviates many such searching problems.

One fun suspended container is the type of wire mesh basket sold in cookware departments for draining vegetables. A deluxe model comes in tiers of three. With a pulley system, these baskets become small elevators for delivering goods to upper bunks.

One mother made simple square bags of sturdy, fine-mesh netting, bound with bias tape and finished with heavy-duty zippers. Tape loops at the top make them easy to hang up. Each bag holds its own specialty, from small cars to cotton socks. (If your child is learning to read, you might want to add simple labels.)

String shopping bags have the same advantage of transparency (we show one in the lower photo on page 11). And as you rush out to the car with your toddler, grab one off the hook to take along for entertainment.

Baskets

From the wicker dish for Baby's cotton balls to the large straw hamper for dress-up clothes, well-constructed baskets are fairly indestructible, as well as versatile. Slide them under the bed for out-of-sight storage. Give a small child a picnic basket with a handle for carrying toys from room to room. An assortment of baskets on a desk top keeps art and school supplies in order. And, hung from one handle on the inside of the closet door, a small basket eases clothing storage. When it's hung low, its contents are easy to see and to reach.

Tidy solutions for clothes & other clutter

Some children, we've been told, are naturally neat and tidy. But most seem to be inclined the opposite way. One parent suggested wryly that kids should have tilting floors: at the push of a button, all the socks, blocks, and other debris would slide into a cavern hidden beneath.

Such a mechanism might prove a little too tricky for most parents to install. Fortunately, there are other ways to help clear up clutter and encourage tidiness. The first ingredient is some thoughtful planning—here are some ideas to help you with yours.

After-school catch-all

When kids come home from school laden with jackets, books, lunchboxes, and important mimeographed bulletins, what do they usually do as soon as they're inside the door? Pile everything in a heap on the first surface they find, whether it is an antique commode in the entryway or a crowded kitchen countertop.

To solve this problem, one family gave their children a network of individual nooks specifically designed to catch such clutter. It works well, because its location, just inside the back door, makes it instantly available to each arriving child.

As shown above, the labyrinth of shelves and alcoves was tucked neatly under a staircase. Adjustable metal brackets make it easy to rearrange shelves or to add more. Coat hooks are screwed to the backs and sides of the lower alcoves.
Architect: George Cody.

Redesign the closet

Children's closets nearly always have a lot of wasted space. You can probably rearrange this space with thoughtful planning to make it store both clothing and toys more efficiently. Given an organized storage space to start with, children are more likely to keep their paraphernalia in good order.

One good way to start is to lower and shorten the clothes pole to suit your child's small stature for several years. In the closet shown below, the shift of a clothes pole yielded room for innumerable shelves and even built-in drawers.

Rainbow graphic transforms the formerly uninspired appearance of plain closet doors. At left, a crowd of cuddly toys clusters on a doll pole — easy to take down, just as easy to put back; for more details, see page 34. Design: Anne Stewart.

Once their cargo was pop bottles and oranges, but today these crates lend their built-in niches to display treasured dolls and miniatures.

Numerous cubbyholes, shelves, and drawers built into the rear of a walk-in closet give a young lady many places to cache provisions like her doll's house and T-shirts.

The pride of ownership... They hung up their shingles

For children, as well as the rest of us, ownership is a source of pride and self-confidence. Usually, their biggest chunk of material wealth is real estate — their own rooms, or portions of rooms. On these two pages, eye-catching graphic designs name the owner of each bedroom with electric clarity.

Besides painted or printed graphics, there are a number of different ways you can give a room its own "monogram." Mount large wooden alphabet letters, such as you might find in a home building supply store, on a wall or door. Or, if you like to sew, stitch and stuff alphabet pillows to spell your child's name — patterns are available from major companies. Then arrange the pillows along your child's bed for both spelling and cuddling.

For a simple and pretty touch, you can decoratively paint, sketch, glue, or embroider the letters of your child's name on a suitable background, then frame your work and hang it in the bedroom.

Annie pours her day into her diary as she relaxes beneath a bold, Broadway-inspired graphic of her name. The screen to the right of her bed is fabric-covered; details appear on page 31. Design: Reo Haynes.

"N" gets a nuzzle for the nice noise it makes in the middle of a very nice name. Design: Reo Haynes.

Nine repeats of his face on the door let everyone know whose private world lies within (please knock). His crisp black and white banner is composed of photographic transfers of his face, block-printed on cotton.

Emphatic-looking on its high shelf, Eric's shingle names with authority the master of this bedroom. The spray-painted plastic letters were found at a hardware store. Design: Mary Martin.

In this apartment-scale bedroom, each bunk opens to its own half of the room (the floor is raised alongside the upper berth). An adjustable shelving system constructed against all four walls allows both storage and flexibility. Though it appears built in, the wall system is actually freestanding and can be disassembled and moved. A large mirror facing the foot of the beds (see detail) creates a feeling of extra space and extends the view of the ceiling mural. Architect: Joseph Kent.

Barn doors faced with redwood benderboard open for extra spaciousness —or close for privacy. Note the pull-out mattresses that hide under the kids' waterbeds, ready for overnight guests. Architect: William Bruder.

Sharing without crowding...Ways to promote peace

The social significance of sharing is a lesson children are taught early in life, first by Mother, then by Teacher. Worthy a lesson as it may be, the average child remains , at heart, as imperious and self-centered as the average 17th century French monarch —especially when it comes to sharing with a brother or sister.

If sharing is the only option, ingenuity in room planning can effectively ease matters. The two key problems are these: how to provide privacy (permanently or temporarily) without cramping, and how to clarify whose space belongs to whom in the jumble of the joint habitat. The following ideas offer some possible solutions.

Part-time room dividers

Siblings —as mercurial as the rest of us —tend to fluctuate between sweet harmony and guerrilla warfare, and sometimes need to be separated for a while. They also need occasional respites of solitude —no matter how they feel about their brothers or sisters.

For both these reasons, a room divider that you can open or close as desired helps to keep peace in a shared bedroom. If the dormitory dimensions are broad enough, you might suspend folding doors or shutters, a cloth or beaded curtain, or even one or more lengthy roller shades from the ceiling. Just make sure that the space doesn't convert into small vertical cells when divided in two, even if the division is only temporary. If that should happen, try instead to arrange the furniture —bookshelves, toy bins, even a bunkbed —to divide the room into territories.

Stretched fabric screen

Stretcher bars, usually used to make an artist's canvas taut, form the quickly assembled frame of a fabric privacy screen (shown in the upper photograph on page 28). When not being used to divide the children's bedroom or to form the walls of a playhouse, the screen folds flat for storage.

Stretcher bars are sold in art supply stores. You may also find them at decorative fabric shops, where they are used to hold fabric panels.

Plan a minimum of three panels for your screen, each no more than 6 feet tall by 2 feet wide.

Buy stretcher bars of the appropriate size, four for each panel, and lock them together at the corners to make each panel frame. Measure the outside dimensions of the frames and add 1 inch to both the length and width. Using tightly woven fabric, sew fabric pieces together into a "pillow slip" for each frame, making 1/4 inch seams, with the opening at the bottom; with the pillow slip wrong side out, box the top corners as shown below.

Fit the pillow slips over the frames, pull the fabric tightly together at the bottom of each frame, and neatly staple it to the frame's bottom. Join the panels, using three hinges —one each at the top, center, and base of each frame juncture.

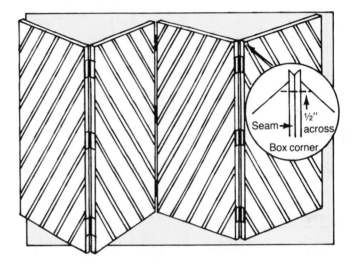

Seam — 1/2" across
Box corner

Personal corners

Young children love to rearrange their own environments to create cozy places —so why not encourage them? Give them lightweight plastic storage cubes (like those shown on page 11), carpet samples, pillows (perhaps one of those shown on pages 42 and 43), and squishy beanbag chairs. When they yearn for a place of their own, let them set up a personal parlor in a corner of their room. Finish off the private nook with a mirror and a bulletin board, if you like.

A paper perimeter

A simple approach to mural painting is to tack up a "stripe" of paper that runs horizontally all the way around the room, positioned so your child can draw comfortably while standing. When it becomes sufficiently embellished, replace it with a fresh strip. Use butcher, shelf, or wrapping paper; newsprint tears too easily. As an alternative perimeter, you might prefer a horizontal stripe of chalkboard paint (see next page).

An easel for two

Long a tradition in kindergarten, a two-sided easel is also very handy for use at home —especially when you have two small artists in the family. Usually, when you set up for poster painting, everyone wants to get into the act.

Here is an easel that you could make for the kids' bedroom or playroom, or for a corner of the kitchen or patio. Its frame is made of hardwood, its backboards are ⅝-inch plywood. The easel's two sides hinge along the top so that they fold together for storage when the wingnuts holding the stabilizing crosspieces are loosened. Two dowels attach each backboard to the frame by fitting into holes in the frame legs: four such holes, spaced at 2½-inch intervals along each leg, make height adjustments possible. The paint shelves are sized to hold square, lidded, plastic refrigerator jars. Design: W. W. Mayfield.

Big, broad paper

If you want to save your wallpaper, here's a wonderful way to deflect youthful artistic zeal to a better "canvas": simply provide an equally generous paper surface on which the children can draw or paint. An exciting size of paper will probably inspire the kids so much that they'll reward you with some very fine artwork.

What sort of paper makes the best substitute for bare wall? From newspaper companies, you can often buy inexpensive rolls of paper that come in widths of up to 55 inches. To sponsor an almost indefinite amount of mural painting, hang one of these rolls on a 2-inch-thick dowel or clothes pole from the pulley-rigged ceiling mount illustrated above. Just pull the artist's "canvas" down and slip it between wood strips that have been screwed to the wall. The strips serve both to keep the mural flat during the creative process and to help you tear the mural off neatly once it's completed.

If you haven't enough wall space to spare, but still want to provide a generous art surface, consider the paper-dispensing table design shown on page 9. Or, from a butcher's supplier, you can purchase a butcher-paper dispenser that bolts to a table or countertop.

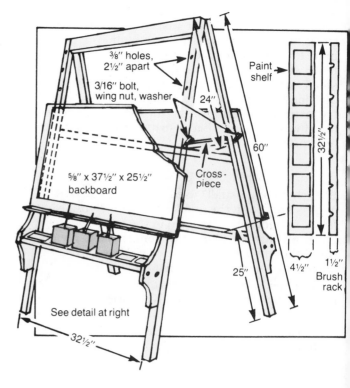

⅜" holes, 2½" apart

3/16" bolt, wing nut, washer

24"

Paint shelf

60"

5/8" x 37½" x 25½" backboard

Crosspiece

32½"

See detail at right

25"

4½"

1½" Brush rack

32½"

How to encourage a young artist's zeal

Before you buy any art supplies for your children's use, check the fine print on the labels for warnings about harmful ingredients. Unfortunately, some products sold for children have been known to contain toxic ingredients. Also, some stain more than others, and some have an unpleasant aroma. If in doubt about the safety of a product, follow the wisdom of kindergarten teachers: buy only water-base flowpens, genuine ceramic clay, and water-soluble powdered tempera paints (which you can thicken, after mixing them, with a little laundry starch).

Practical surfaces

For parental ease of mind, not to mention ease of elbow grease, a child's world should be surfaced with the most readily washable materials available. Naturally, such surfaces make especially good sense wherever kids indulge in arts and crafts, even if that spot is just one corner of the bedroom.

Vinyl wallpaper and floor coverings (the more rugged, the better) are ideal because they mop up with little scrubbing. If you paint the walls or furniture, use several coats of good high-gloss enamel to facilitate cleaning. Decorative plastic laminate, though expensive, holds up admirably atop counters and craft tables, and you can sponge it off with ease.

As an alternative to vinyl, rubber provides a heavy-duty and easy-to-wash floor surface. Janitorial suppliers, among other outlets, offer rubber matting that you could install near an art area. Or consider purchasing a thick plastic mat — the type used to prevent skids at entryways or under rolling chairs — from an office supplier. Lay it over carpeting (which should be a tough industrial or indoor/outdoor variety).

Chalkboards — anywhere, any size, any shape

Today's simple equivalent of the old schoolhouse slate is composed of nothing more than a hard surface well-coated with chalkboard paint (available at paint stores). What this means is that a chalking expanse can go on virtually any surface not needed for other purposes. Perhaps you could convert one side of a chest of drawers, one end of the bunkbeds (or the underside of a Murphy bed; see page 16), or one sliding door of the closet into a chalkboard. Or simply coat a sizable piece of hardboard with chalkboard paint and hang or lean it wherever the artist wishes. With a jigsaw, you can give the board a whimsical contour, like that of the whale shown on page 11. Remember, half the fun of scrawling with chalk is being able to loosen up and spread out, so provide as large a surface as possible.

Construction site

Blocks—those most satisfying and simple toys for builders of any age—deserve a corner of their own. Start a collection with traditional wood blocks from the toy store, adding to it with as wide a variety of safe knickknacks as you and your kids can find. Throw in a few oversize, lightweight blocks made from sturdy gift boxes and food cartons (perhaps covered with contact paper). A few large trucks or an indoor wagon are great for hauling and dumping.

Try to store each construction element—wood blocks, big blocks, and sundries—on its own shelf or in its own labeled bin. The best container is one wide enough so that Junior can easily reach for a few things at a time. For example, the open-front bin described on page 24 makes excellent housing for blocks. Or, if you use large plastic or hardboard cubes to store the blocks, the containers themselves may become part of a small-scale city.

Dolls & stuffed animals

Doll and stuffed animal lovers usually acquire an overflowing collection within the space of their first few birthdays. One mother took the trouble to sew a small plastic ring to the back of each soft friend so that the entire crowd could be hung on cup hooks when not needed for cuddling. She screwed the hooks to a floor-to-ceiling pole.

For children who feel cozier at night with favorite friends nearby, you might provide each doll with its own papoose pocket. Sew straps to each pocket and hang the pockets on a dowel; then suspend the dowel by a pretty ribbon from the wall alongside the bed.

Fooling around on the floor

Children spend so much time there that the bedroom floor deserves an open-minded second glance. While carpeting is definitely the coziest covering, it's best to leave at least a few square feet for vinyl or other smooth flooring where the kids can wheel trucks or set up a doll's house.

Another good idea is to collect a stack of carpet samples from discontinued stock (a very small investment—some shops offer them free of charge). With them, children can make their own patchwork carpet creations or steppingstones—or simply use the samples as comfortable, portable seating.

To the carpet collection, you might add a length of felt, accompanied by assorted felt and fabric shapes and stripes, so the kids can create floor collages.

We've seen designs painted on wood floors—for hopscotch, checkers, tic-tac-toe, and marble games. What about painting foot and paw prints in a path around the perimeter of the room? Or even across it?

Now you see it—now you don't. An inverted drawer slides in and out to give two brothers a smooth play surface for their miniature toys, which might topple on the carpeted floor. More details on their disappearing desk appear on page 17. Design: John E. Mason.

Tuck in a few inviting play places

As we all know from our guidebooks for parents, child's play is a repertoire of important learning experiences. Both a source of relaxation and a very intense kind of work, it gives youth a chance to interpret our confusing world for themselves, in their own terms. If that sounds rather absurdly serious, take heart: play also happens to be fun.

On these two pages you'll find a few ideas for polishing up the play potential of bedrooms, play rooms, or any area in the house where kids can imaginatively create a world of their own.

Spic, span, and sunny, Amy's kitchen resides in one portion of her remodeled closet. Its daintily curtained "window," over the toy stove, is glued to a storybook picture of a formal English garden. Design: Sharon Owen Haven.

Low craft counter along one side of a laundry hall provides plenty of elbow room for finger painting. The blackboard (which the kids reach by climbing on the counter) slides up, disclosing a pass-through to the kitchen. A big laundry sink close at hand (but not shown) makes clean-up easy. Architect: Michael Moyer.

CHILDREN'S ROOMS **35**

Blazing colors (some of them even glow in the dark) depict a world where skyscrapers dance and mountain roads meander right onto the bookcase top. Mural: Jeanne Clark.

Wrapping ribbonlike right around her nursery, Amanda's mural of cats and other furry creatures gives her friends she can talk to, first thing in the morning. Mural: Sidney MacDonald Russell.

Instead of wallpaper...Mural magic

The rich fantasy life of children sometimes kindles the same in their elders. Like shopping for shiny toys or reading Mother Goose aloud, imaginative play gives a grownup the chance to relive a bit of childhood.

One magic carpet to Never Never Land, discovered by a growing clientele of parents, is the superscale "canvas" of a fanciful mural artist. Shown here are a few examples of what can happen to children's walls and ceilings—and even furniture—when you employ one.

To find a muralist, you may have to do some searching. Ask decorators for references, or call art schools and galleries. The young artists whose work appears here include a sign painter, a theatrical set designer, and a high school student.

Dorothy and her mates from Oz parade on high across 5-year-old Jessica's wall, portrayed there by a talented 16-year-old friend. Mural: Nora Escalante.

Splashed across wall and ceiling, bright flowers appear to have taken flight from the print of the bedspread below. Mural: Jackson Art.

Canary-yellow bedsheet puts a bright face over a plain bulletin board wall. Simply thumbtacked in place, it comes down for washing as needed. Design: Sharon Owen Haven.

Waking up walls dignifying doors

Since every square inch of a child's room is at a premium, it's worthwhile to study all surfaces—walls and door-ways, for example—for their potential environmental impact.

Wallpaper is fun, and so are murals—some of which you can buy in wallpaper form. Here on these two pages are a few more unusual treatments for walls and doors—to stir your imagination as you and your kids plan a bedroom face-lift.

Colorful paper patchwork wakes up the wall as it encourages early scholastic skills. Each "patch" was put together on a cardboard square, using contact paper and giftwrap scraps, then discreetly affixed to the wall with four tiny brass nails. Self-adhesive mirror tiles, set into the pattern just atop the storage cubes, add extra delight. Design: Joanne Bowen.

Graphics from one to ten

Big, bold, three-dimensional Arabic numerals, ordinarily used to identify street addresses, might look even more exciting on a child's bedroom wall. Look for them at home improvement centers. Or look in catalogs —we found some lovely rounded numerals in bright green glazed ceramic in a sophisticated home design catalog.

For a preschooler, you might affix the numerals one through ten to the wall in a horizontal row within the junior mathematician's reach. Here, they can be gazed upon, talked about, and even caressed with the fingertips. Perhaps they might bestow some good influence on future money management —or at least toward gold stars on first-grade schoolwork.

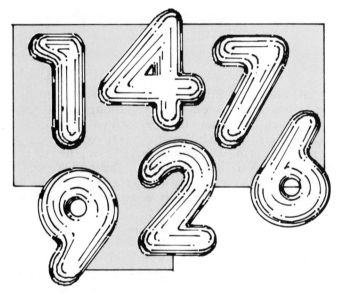

Pin-up mountain range

Bulletin boards generally look rather drab unless well papered with drawings, postcards, and other childish pin-ups. But we saw one that delights the eye —with or without window dressing. Wrapping around three walls, 4 feet high from floor to highest peak, this pin-up board takes the shape of a lengthy mountain chain. Besides the usual paper accumulation, the mountains' owners can pin up their own sketched and cut-out houses, roads, snowmen, trees, and forest creatures.

The mountain range was cut with a saber saw, in very freeform fashion, from 4 by 8-foot sheets of white bulletin board bought at a building supply store. Painted a rich shade of brown and capped with "snow," the peaks call to mind gingerbread with whipped cream as much as they do the Sierra Nevada, the Rockies... or even the Himalayas. Design: Jeanne Clark.

Supergraphic door decor

Bold, bright letters painted on the outside of Steve's and Kelly's doors let the whole world know at a glance whose room is whose.

If you want to try a similar graphic feat, first measure your child's door and then draw it to scale on graph paper. Design block letters within the door outlines on the paper. Short names like Steve or Kelly are easiest to work out in crisp, geometric lettering —but you might run a longer name diagonally.

Scale the letters up to their actual size on wrapping paper (a yardstick helps to keep lines straight). Cut out the enlargements.

Take the door off its hinges, sand it well, and paint it with an enamel undercoat. When dry, sand it again lightly and trace the letters onto the door. Paint both background and letters (maybe in the kids' favorite colors) with at least two more coats of enamel. For the neatest results, use the best brush you can buy.

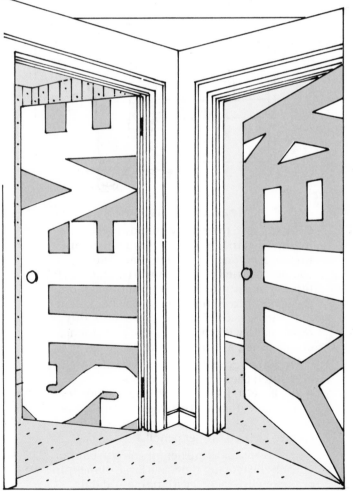

Measurement banner

Children love to see how quickly they're moving upward in life. And a measuring banner invites everyone to stand up and take a look. If you design the banner around two measuring tapes—one divided into traditional inches and the other into meters—you also offer lessons in the mysteries of metric conversion. Buy two tapes, each with meters on one side, inches on the other, at a fabric store.

Design a vertically shaped felt wall hanging and stitch the two tapes to opposing edges. A giraffe with its lofty neck readily lends its proportions to a measurement banner. But you might also choose a "tree trunk"—or a canary-colored "super pencil."

Handy for marking heights on the banner, at each measuring time, is a large diaper pin or paper clip, tagged with name and date.

Fabrications for future citizens

A bright new look with fabric paint

If you are already planning to make bedspreads and curtains for your child's room—had you thought of fabric-painting them? First wait for a department store linens sale; then buy enough full-size sheets to cover everything that needs covering. (Solid color cotton from the bolt is fine, too—but you'll need to sew more seams.) At an art supply store, look for jars of water-base fabric paint—the kind that bonds to cotton cloth as it tumbles at high heat in a dryer.

Whether you, your kids, or the whole family joins the painting fun, plan before you plunge ahead—things can get messy. On paper, sketch a scene you'd like to depict. Or, design and cut out stencils to paint through (large alphabet stencils from a stationer's might create a dictionary or monogram design). For stripes, plan to use guideline strips of masking tape to run your brush along; for polka dots, try a large thread spool, dipped in the paint. And for an interesting screened effect, try painting through a mesh fly swatter.

To begin painting, pin the sheets up on an outdoor wall, protecting the ground, if necessary, with a drop-cloth. Tape any stencils or stripe guidelines in place lightly, so that the sheets won't pucker when the tape is removed after painting. Offer hardware store brushes in assorted widths. Don't remove any taped stencils until the paint is completely dry.

Set the paint by tumbling the sheets in a dryer, on its hottest setting, for 45 minutes. (In later washings, to protect the paint, use cold water with mild soap or detergent.)

After drying, the painted sheets are ready to be made into bedspreads or curtains. (You might find the *Sunset* books *Slipcovers & Bedspreads* or *Curtains, Draperies & Shades* helpful here.)

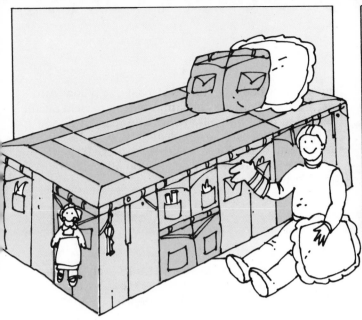

Blue jeans jigsaw bedspread

John's casual coverlet, made with recycled jeans, doubles as a treasure chest and teaching toy. His mother's design includes pockets and belt loops to hold the boy's pint-size riches. Extra fun that came with the jeans are buttons, snaps, and zippers — for exercising preschool skills.

The top of the spread is a patchwork of cut-off jean legs. The entire single-bed-size creation required a dozen pairs of adult-scale jeans, both corduroy and denim.

Card table playhouse

Make a simple cotton duck slipcover for a card table (or any table of similar size), and you'll have the basic structure of a roomy little playhouse.

Seam the top to all four side pieces, but leave the sides detached from one another. Bind all raw edges with bias tape. Attach two 12-inch lengths of tape below each corner, so you can tie the sides together after slipping the "house" over the table.

Decorate the slipcover to please your own whims and those of your kids (unless this is a surprise, they're sure to want to help you). You might appliqué floral print rose bushes, or velveteen shutters, or even a few grazing sheep of fake fur — all with a zigzag stitch.

Doorway puppetry

To inspire spur-of-the-moment puppetry, all you need are a rectangle of cloth, a tension-mounted curtain rod, and a convenient doorway. Cut the cloth to fill the doorway from about half its height to the floor. Hem raw edges, leaving the top hem open at each end and making it wide enough to encase the rod. Ask your child to sit behind the curtain so you can mark the right position for a stage opening. Then cut out a window and bind its edges with wide bias tape. Add a simple curtain (the buttoned-on-type shown here is fun).

Thread the rod through the top hem, fit it between the door jambs — then pop some popcorn and settle back for showtime.

41

Pillows...
For cuddling
in the dark
or in the day

Every bedroom needs at least one pillow. And for anyone in the family who can wield needle and thread, pillows are a snap to stitch. So pile in as many as you please—your kids will hug them, stack them, toss them, cherish them. Here are a few to get your collection off to a smooth and squishy start.

Children's own creations

Give your son or daughter a big pillow-size sheet of paper and ask for a big crayon drawing of a good pillow shape—maybe a favorite animal. Then look for fabric that will correspond to the artist's colors, and use the drawing as a sewing pattern. Transfer details to the pillow front with dressmaker's carbon, and zigzag-stitch them in place. Then seam pillow front to a backing piece, and fatten it with batting.

Tell the kids that drawings with simple contours (like the fluffy white cat shown on the facing page) are the easiest to translate into a pillow.

Kite & windsock pillows

In Japan, children get an annual chance to celebrate the joy of having been born a boy or a girl. On Boys' Day, May 5 (Girls' Day is March 3), one tradition is to fly giant cotton windsocks in the colorful shapes of creatures that live in the sea or in the air —fish, whales, hawks, and moths, for example.

Look for windsocks at Oriental import shops in March or April. The highly popular carp—filled with shredded foam, its mouth and tail stitched closed—becomes a beautiful bolster nearly as long as a child's bed or as wide as a love seat. Since washing will fade the delicate dyes, it's wise to spray the pillow with an aerosol soil repellent.

Boys' Day paper kites are more widely available than cotton the year around, in assorted sizes. Use these as patterns for a multi-colored pillow menagerie.

Funny-face pillow for busy fingers

You can sew a curious face on an 18-inch pillow— a face with a nose that laces, eyes that button, and a mouth that zips. The very young will love to toy with the cheerful gadgetry.

Cut out the pillow front and back, but don't sew them together until you've appliquéd the face. To make the mouth, cut out a pair of luscious red felt lips; join them with as heavy a metal 7-inch zipper as you can find. With zipper closed, appliqué the mouth to the pillow front.

The nose requires two felt strips, each 1 inch wide and 6 inches long; attach a row of three metal eyelets to each. Appliqué the strips to the pillow front, side by side, leaving their inside edges open and unattached. Thread a thick shoelace through the eyelets, and tie it at the top or bottom.

To make pupils for the eyes, sew on two large buttons. For eye variety, cut a number of pairs of felt shapes (such as circles, stars, or hearts in different colors) making a central buttonhole in each that a child can slip over one of the button-pupils. You might give the pillow variable cheeks, too—cutting these from felt in different shapes and colors. To attach them, sew big snaps to the pillow front and cheek undersides.

As a last, realistic touch, sew yarn fringe into the pillow seam on three (or even all four) sides, as you join the pillow front to its back. Then stuff the friend to make it properly plump.

Sleek, slick, and shiny satin surfaces look as delicious as they feel — especially in such soft sculpture shapes as candy bars and crayons.

Boy-size building blocks are actually foam rubber cushions. Joshua can also spread them out to sleep an overnight guest.

"Marshmallow" is a most appropriate name for Mary's humorous cat. Adapted from her own drawing, it is indeed a proud pillow (for details, see "Children's own creations" on facing page).

Jason's head, hands, and knees propel a caterpillar-like "tractor" across the floor.

The joys of piling up & tumbling down

Take a room full of foam cushions, add some small children—and you no longer have a room, but a blizzard of perpetual motion. Most of the motion is silly, and none of it is hazardous at all.

These crazy pillows come in two basic shapes that mesh delightfully when combined—one is a sort of performing seal's platform, the other a caterpillar mat that bends and ties to form a hollow hexagon.

Each shape acts very much like furniture but more closely resembles a squishy, elephantine toy. Stacked up, the shapes become instant soft sculpture to knock down—like a constantly collapsing circus.

What kids love is that the big foam cushions are colorful, lightweight, soft, and bouncy—with endless new uses for young inventors. Here are a few that Hilary, Jason and Xani discovered—in the space of maybe five minutes. Design: Patricia Moser.

Five elephant footstools give Xani a palatial tunnel with guest seating upstairs.

Hilary discovers that her hexagon mat is almost alive . . . at least it wriggles in nearly every direction.

Any second now, their totem pole will topple. Foam pillows stack up high . . . rather unsteadily.

Having corralled her, Jason now puts a lid on her.

When all falls down, you can still leap into the squishy wreckage.

Moonglow from an origami-trimmed lantern sets the mood for Gwynnie's woodwind magic. The young musician sits on a fully opened *shiki-buton*, a Japanese folding bed. (See facing page for more details.)

Sleeping sweet & simple

For reasons that still elude anthropologists, child psychologists, and school board officials, children love to sleep on the floor. They don't care if it's dusty, drafty, or hard on the back.

Maybe the elasticity of youth explains this predilection—after all, kids also wake up without kinky joints after nights passed in hammocks or on airplanes. Or maybe it's simply the refreshment of diversity. For in our portion of the globe at least, parents don't usually permit hammockry or floor-sleeping as a nightly routine.

In any case, it's wise to provide for occasional out-of-bed sleeping—whether for Junior alone on the night of an eclipse, or for a gaggle of slumber-partying 7-year-olds. Here are a few ways to do so.

Soft sculpture glamorizes the wall by day, then comes down at night to bed an overnight guest. The cool satin rainbow and lightning bolt make comfortable sleeping; the storm cloud proffers a pillow. Design: Heidi-Merry.

The *shiki-buton*

The Japanese, who have been sleeping down low for a long time, have devised some very cozy floor accommodations. One that is particularly elegant and versatile has become increasingly available here. Called a "shee-kee-boo-ton," it consists of three foam rubber pads, covered and linked with fabric. It is lightweight and foldable. Besides acting as bedding, it bends into a playhouse or an ottoman. And with one pad extended up the wall, it makes a very nice chair.

A luxurious accessory to a shiki-buton is a thick quilt that rolls up and fits into its own little drawstring duffle bag, to be used during the day as a bolster.

Sleeping on air... indoors or out

Partially inflated with air, a waterbed mattress makes a wonderful floor cushion for guest sleeping. One, two, or even three kids in sleeping bags can fit comfortably on its broad, squishy surface. It can take plenty of roughhousing, too — its hide is tough.

Outdoors, the versatile mattress offers further fun. For a stargazing sleep-out on the patio or lawn, it provides an oversized air mattress. In a swimming pool, it makes a slippery floating island.

With most canister vacuum cleaners, it's easy to fill a mattress with air. Shift the hose into the opening through which air flows out; then hold the nozzle against the mattress opening, turn on the vacuum cleaner, and watch the mattress balloon up (don't let it go too far, though).

A gurgly water filling delights kids, too. But a word of caution: indoors, there may be electrical hazard if you don't also use the frame and plastic liner that go with a complete waterbed. A water filling outdoors is safe, but insulate the mattress with a thick blanket, because the water will get chilly.

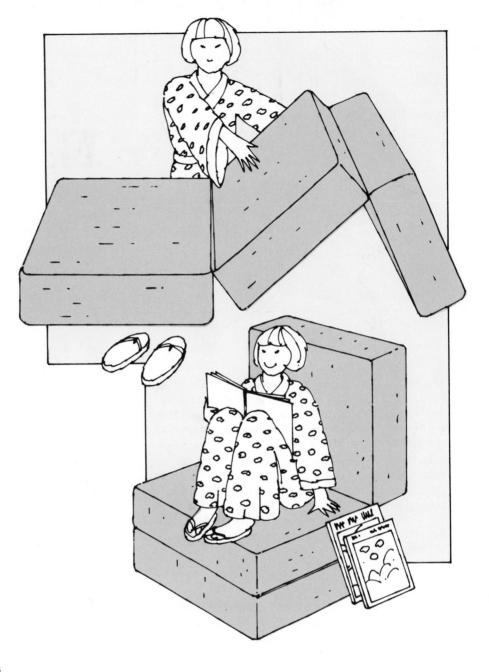

Hammocks

Every home with youthful inhabitants needs at least one hammock, if not half a dozen.

Install hooks for hammocks in your child's room (consult "Anchor it safely," page 57). Leave the hammock permanently in place—or roll it up until it's needed. Left in place, it makes a lounge on which to swing gently with a good book, or it's a place to store toys. Taken down and put away, it leaves the hooks free for other uses, like keeping jackets off the floor.

Swivel chair

Maybe the best feature of the classic swiveling office chair is its built-in capacity to whirl dervishly as well as to roller-skate across a bedroom floor. Most of these chairs also "grow" with a child (maybe all the way to Harvard).

Look for vintage oaken models at used office furniture stores (you may need to replace the casters). Or, if your taste leans more to sleek and contemporary designs, you can find up-to-the minute versions with molded plywood or plastic seats at Scandinavian furniture shops. Some of them are espeoially designed for kids.

Getting up high

It makes good sense to give your son or daughter something safe to stand on when reaching way up for things. Otherwise, the young explorer is bound to get there anyway—regardless of personal risks. At hardware stores, you can buy a tough little drum-shaped step stool whose casters retract under a child's weight, allowing a rubber suction device to grip the floor and steady the stool. Made by several different manufacturers, these are about 14 inches high and surfaced with skidproof rubber treads.

For an older child, you might look into ladders (dealers are listed in the Yellow Pages). Especially interesting is the rolling variety used in libraries, bookstores, and warehouses. Its spring-loaded casters operate exactly like those on the step stool, retracting under an older child's weight so that suction cups grip the floor.

Today's government regulations for ladders are strict, so ladders manufactured for commercial use should be quite safe at home. Remember, though, safety also depends on your child's age and skill.

No-nonsense, good-for-them furniture

Climb-up-to-the-table chair

When your butterball bouncer reaches the age of exploration, the highchair often becomes more interesting to climb into and out of than to sit in and sup in.

Especially if the highchair has become a bit wobbly, it might be a good idea to substitute this wonderful halfway-grownup version. Easily climbable and safely stable on its 24-inch base, its big bonus is holding Baby snug against the table — with the rest of the family.

The chair's curved backrest adjusts to cup a small child closely, and the armrests fit over the table top, to keep wriggly little bodies from sliding out during dinner. When it's time to get down, you loosen two butterfly nuts and slide the backrest away from the table, opening up a wider space through which your child can exit to freedom. You can also bolt the chair's seat at lower positions as the baby grows. Design: Sheldon Smith.

If you are the practical sort of parent who expects a piece of furniture to survive, fairly intact, the enthusiasms of a normally riotous childhood, then maybe you need an especially rugged chest. Or rather, maybe Junior does.

A metal or heavy plastic chest of drawers is likely to fare better than its traditional, often delicately crafted, wooden cousin. Metal tool chests, which sometimes come with heavy casters, will serve the family virtually forever. So will a metal file cabinet from an office supply store. You may want to improve either variety of chest with several coats of bright, high-gloss spray enamel.

A more versatile and less expensive unbreakable chest would be an expandable plastic drawer system which comes in units from shops that feature space-saving furniture.

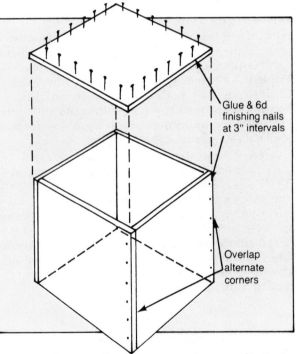

Glue & 6d finishing nails at 3" intervals

Overlap alternate corners

Versatility with solid geometry

Both the cube and its flattened-out cousin, the oblong, lend their shapes to modular furniture systems that are both flexible and fun.

You can buy both at unfinished furniture shops. Usually constructed in 16-inch-deep modules, they are solid enough to hold up for years, yet so inexpensive that you may want to collect a number of them. Paint them with a high-gloss enamel.

With an assortment of button-bright boxes, you and your kids can create (and re-create) an ever-changing environment. Stack them up to make a bookcase, the underpinnings of a desk, or even a condominium for dolls. Or spread them out into a train or a boat.

If you'd like to make your own cubes, use ½-inch plywood—one 4 by 8-foot sheet will furnish you with three 16-inch cubes. For each cube, cut four squares, each 15½ inches on a side, and one square 16 inches on a side. Glue and nail them together, as shown above, with the 16-inch-square piece on top. Sand them smooth and paint them with several coats of high-gloss enamel. (A cube arrangement appears in the lower photograph on page 38.)

Cardboard creations... Sturdy, good-looking & easy

As our tree population dwindles and our lumber prices soar, it becomes increasingly extravagant to supply children with pretty little wooden furnishings that they will soon outgrow. But riding to the rescue of the dollies' tea party comes thick cardboard—a low-cost plywood substitute that has been with us, scarcely noticed, for years. In slabs of three corrugated layers, it is virtually as sturdy as plywood and less than half the price.

Other virtues... & one curable vice

A joyful discovery for the parent who lacks physical strength or carpentry skill, making things with cardboard is much like making model airplanes. Triple-thick sheets of it, which are featherweight to lift, also cut easily with an ordinary breadknife. You can make perfectly adequate joints with interlocking slots, wedged-in supports, and generous applications of white glue and tape.

Keep in mind that, to take stress, the cardboard's corrugated "tunnels" should always run vertically in supporting members. And be wary of the one danger in the craft: cardboard's cut edges are surprisingly and sneakily sharp. Check assiduously to make sure that you've covered all edges left exposed after a piece is finished, using duct tape (or fabric or wallpaper, if you "upholster" your results as shown in the facing photographs). You can find duct tape at hardware stores.

Finding cardboard

It takes some searching by telephone to find industrial-strength, triple-thick cardboard. Look for sources under "Packaging Materials" in the Yellow Pages — some will stock sheets, usually in 4 by 6 or 4 by 8-foot sizes. Most suppliers can order the sheets for you if they don't have them on hand.

Large cartons that package refrigerators are also made of the same corrugated, triple-thick material. You can usually purchase these inexpensively from appliance dealers. Some will even give them away.

Simple table & chairs

A good starting project in cardboard carpentry might be the 20-inch-high table and its 14-inch chairs shown on the facing page.

The table's base is formed by two interlocking legs, joined by slots in the same fashion as many children's construction toys. As illustrated on the next page, one leg has a central slot cut halfway (plus 1/2 inch, for ease of joining) through its height, starting from the base; the other has an identical slot cut from the top. These slots are exactly the thickness of the cardboard—hold the cut edge of a cardboard sheet against the table leg and trace around it to make a pattern for the slot. After you cut the slots, slide the first leg down over the second, and the slots will interlock.

To sketch the table top's circular shape right on the 4 by 4-foot sheet from which you'll cut it, make a compass of scrap cardboard. The scrap should be as long as the radius you desire (ours is 20 inches, and yours can be no longer than 24). Poke a pencil through one end of the scrap and nail the other lightly to the center of the sheet. Swing the pencil end around to draw the circle; then cut the top out and lay it on the floor.

Position the base, its two members spread crosswise, on the table top. Trace the base's position, then glue the base in place. Reinforce it by gluing to the top, and then taping, four pie-shaped wedges, cut from scraps to fit tightly between each pair of legs.

The simplest stool design would be a miniature version of the table. Or you can make boxy chairs like those shown in the photograph. For the latter, you start by cutting and fitting together interlocking bases made of four 14-inch cardboard squares, each with slots on both sides. For strength, cut the slots at least 2½ inches from each side edge (as shown on the next page).

Next, cut a square reinforcing wedge to fit tightly inside the open top of each base, and a seat just big enough to cover the base completely (14 to 16 inches square). Glue each wedge to the center of a seat's underside; then glue and fit the seats to the bases, pressing the reinforcing wedges tightly inside the bases. Reinforce all joints with duct tape.

Each set of chair back and arms was cut from a single strip of cardboard, then scored—cut through just the outside corrugated layer of the strip—where the arms form corners with the back. Joined to the chair seats with glue and tape, these strips are not absolutely essential. They may become wobbly after a few wild tea parties—but they should hold together at least until the chairs are outgrown.

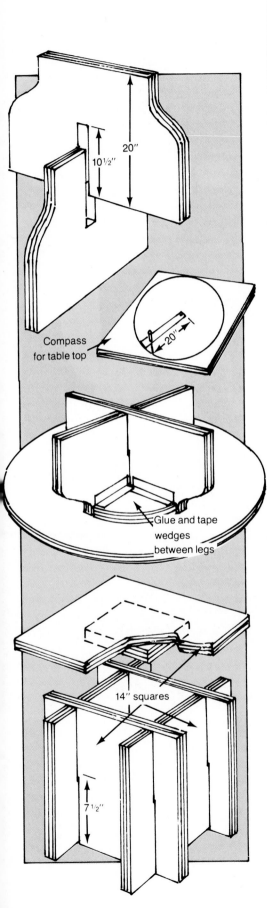

20″

10½″

Compass
for table top

←—20″—→

Glue and tape
wedges
between legs

14″ squares

7½″

Cardboard whimsy for tots or teddy bears fits together with glue, tape, and interlocking slots. Finish furniture (after taping cut edges) with enamel, glued-down fabric (vinyl is waterproof), or wallpaper. Design: Françoise Kirkman.

Puppet theater "hinges" with loops of heavy cord — you can fold it flat for storage. Its spongeable vinyl wallpaper surface makes an excellent overcoat for cardboard. Design: Laura Ferguson.

Heirlooms... Hand-me-downs to treasure

As we scatter ourselves far afield, quickening our pace from one roof to the next, whatever will become of heirlooms? It would be a shame to lose every last bit of bric-a-brac in the shuffle.

While reverence for heirlooms may not prevail today as widely as it once did, many families still pass these treasures along, even to youthful members. Parents feel a special reassurance when their baby sleeps in a cradle that has already comforted generations of family young. To a child, even a small silver trinket that once sat on Great-grandmother's shelf carries with it a sense of belonging and self-worth. Heirlooms engender pride — and a moderate dose of pride won't hurt any of us.

If you have no readily available attic to raid for family treasure, and the romance of heirlooms stirs your fancy, you might start a tradition with your own children. Invest in a bit of history — a chest or a rocker — that they can grow up with and later hand down themselves.

Cradling her mother's (and grandmother's) favorite doll, Zee-Zee reposes on her regally festooned Victorian bed.

Country antiques improve with a few nicks and scratches from service to children. These pieces also happen to blend delightfully with bold contemporary fabrics. Design: Judith Snable.

Little Megan's assorted wickerware has seen four generations' worth of comfortable nursery reclining.

A treasury of dolls fills her cabinet today, but tomorrow—who knows? Rare books, rare china . . . or maybe the very same dolls (a number of which are heirlooms themselves).

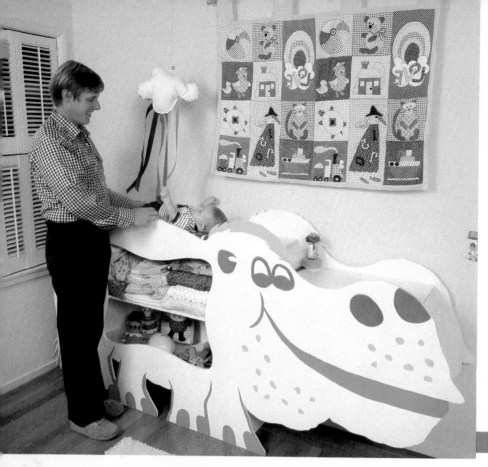

Fat hippo changing table was dreamed up by Timothy's carpenter father and painted by his mother. Storage crannies built into the animal's sides and between its jowls will serve for years, long after Tim has stopped wearing diapers. Design: Andy Andrews.

Fun furniture... For & from the young at heart

While many of today's furniture designs for the young reflect, in miniature, the serious aspirations of adult "good taste," there is no particular reason why they should. Kids are very open-minded about matters of taste. They're also naturally zany —as are many of us parents, under our surface crust.

If strictly functional furniture reminds you more of a chilly boarding school than a happy home, the ideas on these two pages should cheer you up. Here are creations from parents who dared to scale the heights of whimsy as they furnished their kids with the otherwise humdrum necessities of life.

Daddy's darling dines in a very regal throne, indeed. Its painted fantasy tray is not only entertaining to look at, but fun to decorate with cooky crumbs. Design: Sidney MacDonald Russell.

Brian's step-stool gains dignity from a decorative stencil of his name. It proudly bespeaks the owner of this valuable piece of equipment.

Bouncy balloon chairs

Colorful, crazy, and quite cheap to make, these air-filled seats won't last forever — but they do provide quality guest seating for tea parties or musical chairs.

For each pair of chairs, you'll need a sturdy cardboard carton that measures 20 by 23 by 23 inches. You can buy such cartons from moving companies or sometimes pick them up free from appliance dealers. Slice each in half, diagonally, to make two chair frames. Using wide masking tape, cover the cut edges, for they can be surprisingly sharp.

To make the air-filled cushions, you'll need to sew sacks of soft cotton mesh to hold the balloons. Make a 30 by 36-inch sack for the back of each chair, and one or two 24 by 30-inch sacks for each seat. Inflate about 3 dozen round balloons per chair (this allows a few extra for bursting and batting around). For maximum longevity, inflate the balloons just enough to make them firm. Fill the sacks with balloons and close them with string, woven through the mesh and tied loosely so you can free the balloons at the end of a party, or add new ones to replace popped ones.

Improvements with paint & découpage

From fancy showrooms to humble garage sales, our world is clogged with large, squarish articles of furniture that, while serviceable, are completely devoid of whimsy. It's up to parents and kids to improve their sad faces with jars or spray cans of high-gloss enamel in joyful colors. (In some cases, even a few swipes of fingernail polish make a great improvement).

Your decorating options are many. Consider stars, stripes, polka dots, or funny faces. Or follow the contours of the furniture, if they lead you in a fanciful direction . . . turn each drawer into a miniature mural, chair spindles into a rainbow medley.

If freehand painting alarms you, there are other approaches. Borrow motifs from children's books, giftwrap paper, or needlework patterns. Copy these or use them to make stencils (you can buy stencils, too, from a stationer) through which you can brush or spray the furniture. Or try découpage: affix a cutout paper collage, using white glue.

If you paint your furniture, let each color dry thoroughly — 4 to 5 days — to avoid later chipping. When dry, coat either paint or découpage with clear polyurethane varnish for maximum protection. (You might find the *Sunset* book *Furniture Finishing & Refinishing* helpful here.)

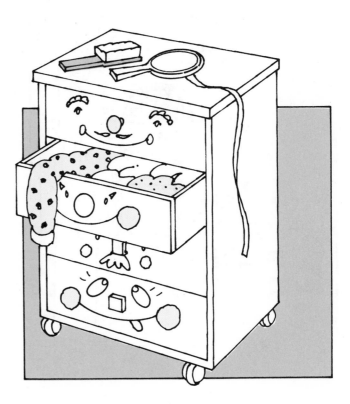

Telephone booth

Teenagers are notoriously long-winded on the phone, but so, very often, are the rest of us — whether the teens are ahead of us or far behind.

While it's easy to appreciate the friendly appeal of Mr. Bell's miracle, in talkative familes the phone location sometimes becomes a rather noisy depot —especially at the busiest times of day.

One solution might be to unplug it and hide it in the linen closet, at least during dinnertime. On the other hand, if that closet — or any other — offers enough space for a lamp, a shelf, some big cushions, and a small bulletin board, you might transform it permanently into a home phone booth.

In such a nook, conversations can ramble on in privacy without your having to overhear every giggle and shriek. Here, too, telephone clutter — pinned-up messages and tattered books — will stay pleasantly out of sight.

Nooks, crannies & other clever little spaces

Flashy laundry chute

Shooting laundry down this big, shiny pipe is much more fun than bother. When not swallowing linens, it also makes an excellent echo chamber — for ghost voices in the basement.

One family's chute was pieced together from lengths of 18-inch-diameter galvanized heating duct that extend it from the owners' first floor to a laundry basket in the basement below. Its top is an 18-gauge adjustable elbow joint: it looks like a ship's funnel.

To find duct pipe, look in the Yellow Pages under "Furnaces" or "Sheet Metal Work" — or check with a plumbing contractor. Pipe lengths are crimped at one end, allowing one to fit snugly into another. The seams of both elbow and pipe sections should point downward, so that clothing won't catch as it tumbles through. Cover any rough spots with furnace tape. Architect: Daniel Solomon.

Alcove gymnastics

Even in a very small home, you're likely to find a few spare inches for a trapeze or chin-up bar.

Nellie's trapeze hangs in an open walk-through between the kitchen and dining room of her none-too-spacious city apartment. When the grownups are having a dinner party, it can be raised to the ceiling, out of the way. Hooks, placed just inside the eyebolts that anchor the trapeze to the doorway header, hold its chainlinks above head height. (See "Anchor it safely," below—Nellie's trapeze did come down when a grownup guest tried it once.)

Anchor it safely

How safely can you suspend chains or ropes from your ceiling to hold the ever-increasing weight of a child? Rugged hardware, deeply esconced in a joist or header, should be safe enough for all suspended delights, from cradle to swingseat. But there is no guarantee that whatever you hang up won't, with time and abuse, come tumbling down—perhaps under the stress of a mature and weighty guest. Also, keep in mind that nylon rope is just as strong as chain—and safer. Another safety precaution is to try your child's equipment under your own weight from time to time.

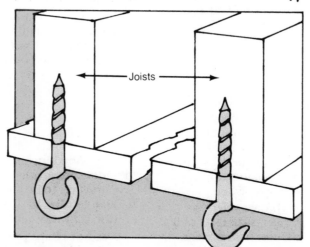

Joists

If you plan to hang anything, the first step is to find a ceiling joist or beam in which to anchor it solidly. Joists always run in the same direction, parallel to at least one wall of a room. Often hidden behind plaster or gypsum board, they are usually spaced 16 to 24 inches apart.

Locations will be easy to discover, and measurements to take, if you have access to an attic where these stocky timbers remain exposed. If you don't, knock firmly on the ceiling with the heel of your hand to find them. Starting from one corner of the room, working in both directions, space your soundings at the likely intervals mentioned above. A solid thud means you've found a joist; a hollow sound tells you to keep hunting.

No matter which method you choose, always doublecheck by drilling a tiny hole through the ceiling, or tapping in a tiny nail, to be sure of striking solid anchorage. If your ceiling is plaster, you may strike only 1/4-inch lath at first, so penetrate a bit further to check for a joist. Use the same method to locate wall studs.

The simplest attachments for chains or ropes are large, heavy-duty eyebolts or ceiling hooks. The deeper and more tightly they penetrate the 6 to 8-inch joist, the longer they will stay put. Screw the hook or eyebolt far enough in so that its curve rests snugly against the ceiling.

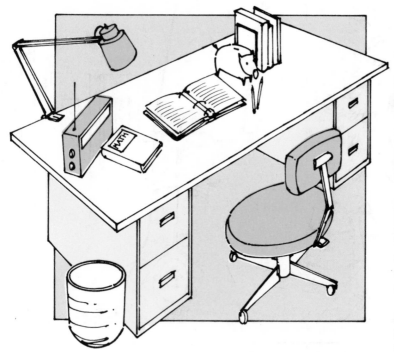

Setting up for study

Sooner or later, homework makes inroads into the evenings of every school girl or boy. Tiresome a chore as it sometimes becomes for both parent and child, once homework starts, it generally doesn't let up for years. It's best to accommodate it as comfortably as possible. If you're lucky, you and the kids may even learn to enjoy it.

Many students do their homework on the living room sofa or spread out in front of the TV. But it may help to ease the task if you give them desks of their own — as well lighted, quiet, and spacious as possible. (Remember that littler kids, who breeze in after school blissfully free of such burdens, like to have their own desks or tables, too.)

Desk tops from doors

Available inexpensively in widths as narrow as 18 inches, hollow-core doors offer ample spread-out space when used as desk or counter tops.

If their standard 6-foot, 8-inch length is too much, doors can be cut down to smaller proportions. But this is a tricky job for anyone but an experienced woodworker with power tools. After slicing it, you must dig out a honeycomblike substance that fills its hollow, then replug the edge by gluing and inserting a cut-to-measure strip of wood.

On the other hand, a full-length door offers so much elbow room for on-going projects that it is well worth while to accept its bulk, if you possibly can.

Before choosing underpinnings for the desk, explore today's interesting array of modular storage units, with your child's size in mind. These units come in various sizes, made of wood or plastic. You can even buy drawer systems that stack — allowing the desk to "grow" with its owner. Young children need a height of about 20 inches. But around the age of 8 or 10, they'll feel more comfortable at a standard adult desk (29 inches high). At that time, you might buy a desk pedestal from an unfinished furniture store — or look for used, two-drawer office filing cabinets, possibly at an office supply warehouse sale.

Whatever supports you choose, it's safest to secure them to the desk top with molly bolts, even though the door is heavy and unlikely to wobble.

Desk lighting

Though Abe Lincoln grew up to become a most wor[n] President, renowned to every school boy and girl, he also grew up to be a very melancholy soul. It may ha[ve] had something to do with reading books by candlelight in a murky cabin.

Eyes work hard when they focus on a printed page — and arithmetic problems sometimes take long staring. To ease things, try to arrange two light sources to illuminate your child's work, with shafts of light cast from either side. This usually means combining a good adjustable desk lamp with the overhead light. Tilt the lamp so that it casts neither shadows nor glare and doesn't shine in the young student's eyes. (Your child may or may not take all this seriously, but explain it anyway.)

Probably the best lamp to buy is the clamp-on type sold by art suppliers and stationers. From base to wide metal shade, it articulates in nearly every direction.

Also, don't neglect a reading lamp by the bed. It is particularly welcome near shadowy lower bunks. Clip-on types attach neatly to bed posts.

A raised, carpeted island — for comic books or floor games — separates individual desks, each assembled from Parsons tables and freestanding drawer units. Design: Sharon Owen Haven.

A pocket of tranquillity, brightly lighted by recessed lamps, makes it easier and more pleasurable for a serious student to concentrate.

On bouncy days, in boisterous weather... Three cheers for playrooms

Bold graphics in circus colors, brightly illuminated from above, transform a previously unused basement into a playroom. The expansive blackboard, cut from masonite, is bordered by bulletin board. Design: Don Merkt.

With rainy days and weary winters, tempers sometimes start to fray from cabin fever. Kids wax fretful, wriggly, whiny. Parents' temples throb...

These are times when a playroom can magically transform misery into merrymaking. Even if nothing more than a carpeted chunk of attic space, a playroom is at times a heavenly haven for all concerned. Here, kids can explode as noisily as they please—and you don't have to hear every decibel of the din. Here, they can churn up a chaos of fun without cluttering everyone else's path—and without having, necessarily, to tidy everything up before bedtime.

While a playroom is perfectly well equipped with such thrifty toys as grocery cartons and inner tubes, you may want to add luxuries later, like a honky-tonk piano or computerized horse-racing.

Wild and whimsical, this playroom features such wonders as a painted piano and a skyward-leaping horse. Behind the curved curtain, the floor was raised to make a stage. Design: Jeanne Clark.

Sled of vinyl flooring sample careens down the sloping floor of a rumpus room that appeared, as if by magic, when the roof line was raised during remodeling. Architect: George Cody.

Comfortably close by, Mama's little ones can call "Watch me!" through the open interior window between kitchen and playroom. She, in turn, can keep an eye on them while she cooks. Architect: James Caldwell.

A little imagination makes life a lot more fun

One of the sweetest charms of youth is its imagination. One of the bonuses of parenthood is getting cajoled into joining a few flights of youthful flamboyance. And one of the most resourceful laboratories for imaginative genius is the family dwelling.

Parents do vary in the degree of imaginative fervor that they find charming or tolerable. Some mothers will crochet a red Santa Claus suit for the TV to wear at Christmas; others will not. Some will allow rhubarb pizza for breakfast; others find eggs and oatmeal too sacred a routine to disturb.

But wherever we can fit a dose or two of imagination into our kids' bedrooms and play places, it's likely to add vigor and cheer to the average household atmosphere.

Hat rack occupies only a few inches of wall space in a small, shared bedroom. But in return, it offers these preschoolers a shape-matching puzzle board as well as all kinds of elegant head gear. Design: Anne Stewart.

Monkey limbs and a firepole give Kevin instant access — faster and funnier than stairs — to the kitchen. He and his brothers have the strongest muscles for miles around. Design: Jocelyn Baum.

Fanciful windows

The reasons for blocking out windows are generally of a practical nature. In cold weather, you probably want good, insulative coverings. If your child becomes frightened at night by inky glass or outdoor shadows, of course you'll want to shut out the goblins with curtains or a shade. And in some room situations, children need privacy — just as adults do.

But, if none of these conditions apply, you and your kids might enjoy a refreshing switch from traditional window coverings. One that delighted us consists of several horizontal rows of clothesline. Suspended by clothespins from the lines are an assortment of colorful children's knee socks — the odd socks that we all accumulate, either because the children outgrow them or, more often, because their mates get swallowed mysteriously by our automatic driers.

Another, rather romantic treatment is to suspend ribbons — matched, coordinated, or mixed up—from the window top. Sew a variety of objects to the ribbon ends to prevent runaway fluttering — a few bells, some shells, wood spools, brass washers…

Your kids can arrange a "stained glass" mosaic on the window if you supply them with white glue, colorful tissue paper, and thin, translucent vinyl from an upholstery or auto supply shop. Just scissor the vinyl into interesting shapes, each about 4 to 6 inches square, then glue the bright tissue paper to them. The vinyl mosaic "tiles" will adhere to clean glass when pressed in place (they don't stick very well if the window is damp); for later rearrangement, they simply peel off.

Photographic foolishness

Delight in one's own appearance is pandemic among youth (maybe among the rest of us, too, even when we pretend otherwise). And photographic wonders also seem to have a universal appeal.

Combine these two delicious truths, add a liberal helping of imagination — and you come up with "photographic foolishness," a zany kind of interior decor with numerous applications.

One source of this kind of fun is turning up with increasing rapidity at amusement parks: computer booths with machines that spew forth space-age camera likenesses for a moderate fee. These photos lend themselves beautifully to artistic improvement with colored pencils.

Kids also love superscale blowups of themselves. First, you need to take a memorable photograph — maybe an action glimpse of your child racing across a field, or a more formal pose in elaborate costume. Take the portrait's negative to a photographic laboratory for enlargement as a poster of exciting size. Any lab can make a black-and-white poster from black-and-white or color film; for color results, you may have to search through a photography magazine for a sophisticated mail-order supplier.

Affix the poster to a wall where it will have the most impact — or to the outside of the bedroom door, where it might startle the unsuspecting passerby right out of his shoes.

Waterworks

A long time ago, most well-appointed bedrooms had their own sinks. Today, the very idea may appall you at first — because of the expense, if not because of potential spills. But if you can install a sink in your son's or daughter's room, once either is old enough to avoid watery catastrophes, it is sure to be greatly appreciated.

People of any age are soothed and fascinated by water. An extra sink has practical value, too — it will save both commotion and soapy surfaces in the bathroom. As a versatile piece of play equipment, a handy sink encourages water colors and good grooming, sailing boats and mixing potions, bathing the dog or a rubber dolly, even brushing teeth and cleaning the goldfish bowl.

Choose a sink with an ample rim or, even better, counter space around it; install vinyl flooring below. For advice on home installation, consult the *Sunset* book *Basic Plumbing Illustrated*.

Keeping creatures

Parents' views on pet life in the bedroom vary as widely as do their views on everything else. But to children, pet appeal is nearly universal. Even if you already have family dogs and cats, sooner or later your kids will probably want to adopt something tiny and strange of their very own.

If you're squeamish about strange creatures, it won't stunt your kids' growth to forego keeping them indoors. And some pets should be banned for safety's sake; turtles sometimes carry an infectious disease called salmonella, and little friends captured in the garden may be tainted if you've used poisons outside.

Safer and more traditional are the creatures sold at pet stores. Easiest of all to care for, probably, are hardy fish such as goldfish and guppies. Infants and young children delight in them.

But older kids may find fish rather lacking in personality. In such a case, you might want to try either a guinea pig or hamster (they reproduce sometimes if you buy two), or mice or rats, if you can tolerate them. Assure yourself beforehand that Junior will handle all feeding and cleaning — rodents can be appallingly messy.

Wildlife in the bedroom — Pets & plants

Indoor gardens

If house plants lend cheer to the kitchen windowsill ...if we adults go a bit overboard in our adulation of a Boston fern...then imagine the wonder and delight that a little growing greenery will bring to a child.

The kind of plant that you and the kids select should depend on how far they have progressed toward the age of responsible garden-tending. It's best to stick to hardy plants that aren't likely to expire or droop disappointingly—aspidistra, devil's ivy, or sansevieria (also called "snake plant") are good choices.

Weird plants—cacti (provide gloves), succulents, the voracious Venus fly trap, or the sensitive plant, which curls its leaves when touched—have a special appeal to young gardeners. You may need to order these types from a plant catalog.

Small children appreciate the broader botanical adventure of starting their own greenery from fruit and vegetable scraps.Soak citrus seeds overnight, then tuck two or three into a container of potting soil; water every few days, and watch them sprout on a sunny windowsill. Or cut about 2 inches off the top of a carrot or beet; trim the leaves off, too. Place the top, cut side down, in a shallow dish containing about half an inch of water. Change the water every

other day. When roots appear, plant the vegetable in a pot filled with moist sand; keep it well moistened on a sunny sill.

A child's house plant becomes an even greater source of pride when you also make a project of choosing and decorating its container. Spread white glue on a plain clay pot, let it dry out a little, and your child can create an elegant mosaic from an infinity of things that might stick onto it: macaroni, beans, shells, beads, bottle caps, old postage stamps, and on and on. Other interesting containers include decorated juice cans, cut-down milk cartons, outgrown tennis shoes, and discarded cowboy hats.

You can increase the pleasures of indoor gardening by arranging a fantasy landscape in a wide, shallow container. If it lacks drainage holes, line the base with a 1-inch layer of horticultural charcoal. Top that with potting soil to fill the pot to within 1 inch of its rim. Then plant an assortment of small-scale greenery with shallow root balls (young plants, sold in 2-inch pots, are about the right size). Add details to delight: miniature animals and buildings, tiny plastic people, perhaps a pocket mirror half buried in soil to simulate a pond (put ducks on it).

Room enrichment: Of endless possibilities, here are just a few

Whether your son or daughter is a reasonably good housekeeper or the more common sweet-but-untidy type, you're bound to find yourself poking around your child's room from time to time. Maybe you're there only to deliver clean T-shirts. Or maybe to hazard a peek under the bed for a lost rubber boot. Whatever your entry ticket, a quiet and solitary tour of the room can yield a bounty of good ideas for room enrichment.

Look around—soak up the atmosphere. It may give you clues to your child's phase of the moment, to needs and enthusiasms that fail to surface clearly in other ways. Start taking notes... room enrichment can happen at Christmas, for a birthday, or any time in between.

Mechanical wonders

If we grownups rely on digital watches and pocket calculators to wend our way through an intricate world, our kids are bound to wish for a few fascinating devices of their own. And many of those sophisticated gadgets make fine room accessories for our young.

When the daily school routine starts, every child learns the down-to-earth meaning of clock time. Mornings may pick up their own smooth momentum if the young scholar possesses his or her personal alarm clock. A big wind-up type is least expensive, and there's something soothing and self-regulatory about winding it up every night at bedtime. On the other hand, many kids find the electrical, digital style of clock more exciting.

Christmases and birthdays offer opportunities to equip a child with items like a flashlight (with extra batteries) to keep at bedside; a mechanical pencil sharpener; and measuring devices, from metal compasses and rulers to room thermometers—especially those that uncloud the mysteries of metric conversion.

A good typewriter will delight a young reader and writer—even one who is still exploring the ABC's. One father found a decades-old model, made entirely of metal, at a thrift shop. Reconditioned for his son's fourth birthday, the typewriter came at a total cost below that of a less rugged (and less grown-up) plastic machine from the toy store.

Crazy day rescue box

Tuck this box out of sight and reach, on an upper closet shelf in a young child's room. It comes down only when you both need instant rescue from boredom or blues—during a sick day, a rainy day, or any garden-variety difficult day.

Stock it as you please with whatever you think will fascinate and delight. You might stash away a few books and toys right after a super-abundant Christmas if you can get away with it. It's a good place to stock interesting craft items, too—buttons, pipe cleaners, yarn, and fabric scraps, to name a few. And don't forget scissors, tape and white glue.

Gentle geography

For a school-age child (especially in the middle years), maps become fascinating to explore. Now is the time for a globe, if you don't already have one in the house.

Or you might provide a diverse collection of maps—a wall-size "atlas." Punch (and reinforce) holes in the upper corners of the maps and hang them on the wall, on cup hooks. They can be interchangeable, depending on the occasion for geographical exploration: before taking a plane trip to another state, when talking about forebears or foreign visitors, bringing to life a social studies assignment, learning the geography of one's own county, or exploring the topography of an upcoming mountain trip.

A little extra color, a little extra light make for brighter and jollier surroundings. Here are stimulating splashes: a plastic Mother Goose lamp (purchased at a toy store) and an ABC night light built with blocks by a fond and industrious mother; fluttery cloth and paper kites to float from the ceiling; an alphabet fabric panel, mounted on artists' stretcher bars; and a plastic-coated chart depicting various crusty characters who dwell in the sea.

Classic technology clusters around an intriguing—if still costly—newcomer: a home computer. Instruments shown here are (left to right) a globe, a barometer, a thermometer that dispenses weather information in both Celsius and Fahrenheit, and a battery-operated clock. The computer broadcasts math exercises via the family TV (it can also straighten out a parent's tax confusions).

Play Yards

The outdoor world exhilarates children immediately—and most of them leap at any chance they get to explore it. Even a vacant lot full of nothing but weeds and a few pieces of junk is, to them, full of interesting possibilities.

Children's outdoor play varies endlessly, and what we present in this chapter offers only a bare glimpse of the full panorama. For example, we haven't touched on some of the more delightful experiences that require no special equipment or adult involvement whatsoever: grinding dandelions for mud soup, discovering animals in cloud formations, making friends with a climbable tree, collecting creatures, chalking on sidewalks, throwing snowballs, or just standing under an umbrella to sniff the rain.

What we have gathered here, instead, are a few good ideas for beefing up the potential of backyard and playground fun—in ways that parents can manage better than can kids left to their own devices. Coincidentally, of course, this also means fostering their physical and mental development. But much as this may matter to us, it's good to remember that our kids are interested only in having a wonderful time.

We've included many safety tips throughout these next pages for minimizing the likelihood of play yard accidents. But risk-taking is a big part of children's outdoor fun, and some children seem to be insatiable daredevils. So safety outside the house is really something that we adults can only aim for, and then hope for. It's wise to be prepared with grounding in first-aid techniques.

Who could resist scrambling into the arms of an old, spreading oak tree—especially when one or two dip invitingly to the ground?

Sand...
One of life's earliest & sweetest pleasures

Why is sand so universally loved by children from the day they first discover it? Because it feels so good and does so much. Dry, it is tinglingly grainy to the touch, yet soft and soothing at the same time. Wet, it turns malleable and gooey, like its equally beloved cousins, mud and clay. Either way, sand is sheer delight to the fingers and toes—especially those of kids between ages two and six.

As the captain scans the horizon, the first mate casts a line into the leafy sea in hopes of catching some supper. Benderboard wrapped around six weatherproof posts forms the hull of their elegant craft, which includes a sandbox between fore and aft decks. Design: Scott Fitzgerrell.

Bright yellow striped canvas shelters kids from a hot summer sun. It also unsnaps to lie right over the sand as a screen against pets.

Sand gadgetry

Though hands and even feet are wonderful tools themselves, a collection of interesting implements will add immeasurable fun to sand play. Search garage sales and thrift shops for big spoons and ladles, fancy molds, strainers, colanders, funnels, coffee pots, and assorted pans. At home, you can make a generous sand scoop, cutting it out of a plastic jug container (thoroughly rinsed and its cut edge covered with plastic tape). Some large toy dump trucks and earth-moving equipment will add to the fun.

Sand without water is as short-changed as peanut butter without jelly. Be sure to provide at least a partially filled bucket or watering can—or, better yet, a quietly dribbling hose.

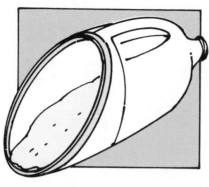

What kind, how much & where to find it

Ocean sand is said to be more hygienic than river sand, but the availability of either, of course, depends on where you live. Do ask for coarse washed sand, best for molding and least likely to be carried into the house on clothes and toes. Especially handy for adding to an already filled sandbox are sacks of about 100 pounds, containing about 1 cubic foot apiece. You can buy these from a lumber or garden supplier and from some toy stores.

A better plan, if you're filling a large sandbox for the first time, may be to buy in bulk and have the sand delivered. (Besides, it's fun to watch the dump truck.) To figure how many cubic feet you need, multiply the length and width of the sandbox by about two-thirds the sandbox depth. Be generous—for decent digging, the sand should be at least 12 inches deep.

Cleaner & dirtier substitutes

Small children adore dirt and mud at least as much as sand, an affection that needn't cause too much alarm for parents. Mudpies are an early childhood enrichment well worth a few spatters on the corduroy.

At the other extreme, pea gravel is as pure and clean a sand substitute as the most fastidious parent could wish. The tiny river-polished stones don't squish as pleasingly as sand or mud, but neither do they cling to clothing or attract cats. Like sand, pea gravel comes either in small sacks containing 1 cubic foot each—or, more dramatically, in a dump truck.

Corralling the sand

A container for sand or pea gravel needn't be fancy. One big tractor tire, its opening widened with a saw, makes a wonderful corral. Kids can sit around its resilient rim, and they'll love to burrow in its recesses.

On the other hand, more elaborate sandboxes (like those shown on the facing page) are often as much fun for parents to build as they are for children to play in. And roominess invites socializing.

Modest or baroque, any sandbox needs adequate drainage, most easily achieved by putting a layer of gravel at its base, over the bare ground. Either place the box in partial shade or provide a canopy or beach umbrella. Screens to keep sand clean are discussed on the next page.

uper sandboxes...
Some parents' happy refinements

Slide-out sandbox cover

Even a small child can slide this cover into or out of its adjoining planter platform. The platform is framed at front and rear with redwood 2 by 12s, the sandbox cover with 2 by 6s. Tops of both are 1 by 2-inch redwood slats. Design: Jerome Gluck.

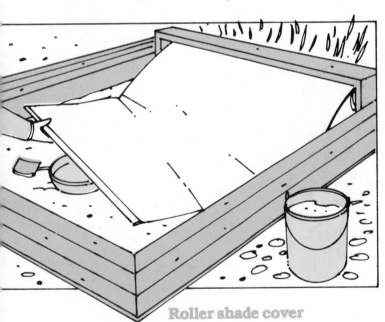

Roller shade cover

A vinyl-coated canvas roller shade shields the sandbox shown above from pets and leaves. (For tips on making your own roller shade, see the *Sunset* book *Curtains, Draperies & Shades.)*

The metal shade brackets, which are mounted at one short end of the sandbox, face inward so the slots that receive roller-points can face upward. A 2 by 6-inch board that hides the roller doubles as a bench. Design: H. Flint Ranney.

Sandbox doubles as play table

This neat little redwood sandbox has its own boxy lid that, when in place, forms a play table, garden seat, or plant stand.

When a big palm outgrew its bed in a paved patio, one family transformed the bed into a sandbox for their two small children. First they dug out about 6 inches of soil and lined the bottom of the bed with bricks for drainage. Concrete footings (about 6 inches deep) set at each of the four corners anchor 6-inch-long metal straps. The inside of the 32 by 36-inch sandbox frame—four redwood 2 by 12s butted at corners—fastens to the straps with woodscrews.

The 1 by 4s of the removable lid are nailed to a 2 by 2 lip on all sides and rimmed with mitered 2 by 3s.

To help keep splinters away, it's important to sand all surfaces thoroughly.

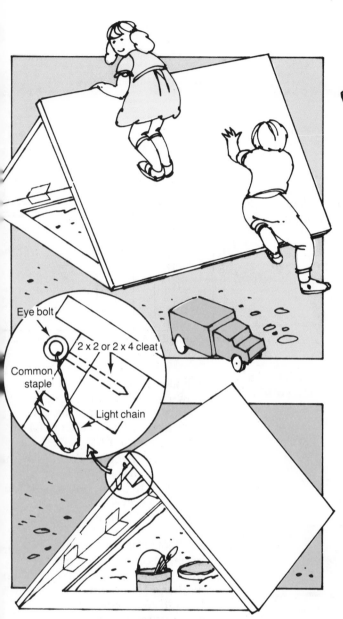

Wide rim makes bench

A good bench wrapping around all four sides adds to the fun of a sandbox. It offers comfortable seating or, when kids sit in the sand, a drag strip for toy cars.

The wide bench shown above is open underneath, making it easy to sweep spilled sand from the surrounding patio back into the recessed sandbox. After its young owner outgrows sand play, the box can become a planter for a tree.

Sand canopy supports swing

Since sand play is often most appealing in warm weather, a sun screen of some sort usually makes sense—unless the box is well shaded by trees. As shown below, the support for a sun canopy (made of lath or a bamboo shade) can carry a small child's swing at the same time—doubling the fun of the sandbox. Design: Thomas Gallup.

Climbable, slideable playhouse cover

Hinged panels of 3/4-inch exterior plywood give this super sandbox a peaked roof to shelter children from sun or rain. It's also a lot of fun to climb up and slide down the plywood "hill" between sand scenes. Several coats of exterior grade paint should prevent splinters.

To form the peak, one 3 by 6-foot panel butts against a 2 by 2 cleat on a 4 by 6-foot panel. The two are secured together as shown above. Heavy galvanized hinges affix each to the sandbox frame (fasten hinges with bolts and T-nuts, making sure ends of bolts do not protrude). When laid flat, the two panels provide a good surface for dumping loads of sand or baking sandcakes. Design: Rick Lambert.

Watery wonders, from patio wetcakes to lawn skidding

On a blazing summer afternoon, what could be more delicious than a backyard soak or splash? Kids turn into seals, wise enough to know that the best way to stay cool is to stay wet.

But even in cold weather, water never ceases to fascinate. Just washing their hands before dinner, little kids linger in blissful oblivion. Even when they're older and more sophisticated, few can resist the allure of a rain puddle or (if they're lucky enough to find one) a brook full of tadpoles.

As we grownups are very much aware, of course, water can also cause tragedy. Even a few inches is enough to drown a small child who trips and panics. Wading pools must *always* be emptied when no one is around to keep an eye on them.

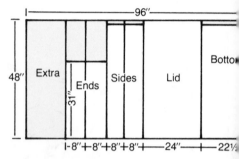

Water slide

Here's the only equipment needed for a riot of slippery glee: a large polyethylene sheet (commonly available as a dropcloth where paints are sold), a lawn, and a garden hose. First you wet the plastic thoroughly—if there's a dip in the lawn, it will become a wide, shallow lake. Then you simply run and skid across it, in any sliding posture that appeals, while your friend tries to zap you with the hose.

While there is little danger of drowning on a soppy polyethylene sheet, there is definite danger to the health of your lawn if you don't move the plastic to a fresh area after an hour's sliding.

Sand-water-clay table

To make the versatile rolling table shown opposite, you'll need a 4 by 8-foot sheet of 3/4-inch exterior grade plywood, plus 8 feet of 4 by 4 standard fir for legs.

Cut the plywood according to the diagram above; attach side and end pieces to the bottom with glue and woodscrews (end pieces will extend 3-1/2 inches at each side). Cut the 4 by 4 into four equal lengths for legs; attach these with carriage bolts, placing two through each 3-1/2-inch extension mentioned above and two more through each basin side into each leg. Countersink exposed ends of nuts and washers to prevent scratches. Drill a drain hole at least 3/4 inch wide in the basin bottom (which you plug tightly from the inside with a cork).

For clay play, cover the lid with canvas or oilcloth, stapling edges to the underside. The lid simply lifts on and off. For indoor-outdoor rolling, add heavy-duty casters.

Finish the table with several coats of exterior paint or polyurethane varnish; waterproof the basin with three coats of fiberglass resin.

Soothing sand at their fingertips, in the basin of this roll-everywhere table, absorbs their attention for hours. Adding water, they can make rivers and lakes—or sandy slush, the basic ingredient for patio wetcakes. Later, a canvas-covered lid turns the sand-water basin into a clay table (canvas removed, the table could further serve as a woodworker's bench). Building directions appear on the facing page. Design: Scott Fitzgerrell.

Simplest of climbers may look like nothing more than a boarded-up sawhorse, but, to kids, it's whatever they need at the moment—such as an Italian racing car or a galaxy cruiser. Design: Sam and Rita Eisenstat.

Tilted cube, with three links missing, makes an elegant climber for a crowd of clambering kids. Design: SunSeeker Cubes.

For scaling heights, here are backyard mountains

Quite early in life, the lure of getting up there beckons as irresistibly as Everest.

To small people, a challenging climb holds out tasty rewards: delicious muscle-stretching, proud mastery of scary situations, the heady thrill of towering above a world that normally towers above them. While they do all that purely for fun, climbing also significantly rewards their development—physical and mental, simultaneously.

Hazard, of course, is part of the experience—for daredevils, the best part. But you can scale down the actual risks when you build a backyard jungle gym. It needn't be taller than 6 or 8 feet to allow for triumphs. Cushion the ground with about a 12-inch layer of soft material (choices are listed on page 80).

To discourage scrapes and splinters, select lumber that has no cracks; sand it well and seal it against splitting from weather changes; round the corners and countersink all connective hardware. Unless spaced and braced for good stability, set upright members in at least 2 feet of concrete.

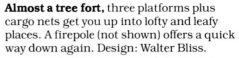

Almost a tree fort, three platforms plus cargo nets get you up into lofty and leafy places. A firepole (not shown) offers a quick way down again. Design: Walter Bliss.

Three ladders take you up to a bridge (a good place to play Three Billy Goats Gruff) with ample elbow room beneath for a tire swing. Design: Sam and Rita Eisenstat.

Gymsets: Play versatility in compact space

Not long ago, the rhythmic creak of a rusty swingset was a common note in the typical suburban cacophony. But in our times of consumer sophistication, the big metal backyard toy has fallen into some disfavor. One reason may be that fingers have been pinched after children grew bored with its routine motions and tried to expand the swingset's potential.

The great thing about a swingset, on the other hand, is that it steals very little space from other backyard enterprises, like vegetable gardening or patio picnics. Here are a few alternative structures —call them "gymsets"—that use up about the same minimal square footage (or very little more). But within their compact design are wide worlds of physical adventure.

Safe swingset alternative features a fat, soft inner tube swing; cotton climbing ropes; trapeze bar; rope ladder; and, at top, a horizontal ladder to crawl across. Design: Developlay.

She tightrope walks a smooth log affixed to a side yard "gymset." Notched log at left leads to a slide at far end.

A small world

Tucked into a garden corner, this small structure built of 4 by 4 posts and 2 by 6 railings offers immense diversity. On either side of a low platform are a 4-foot-wide slide and a ramp with climbing rope. Kids can also swing in a big inner tube, hang upside-down from a horizontal ladder, or do gymnastic tricks on a turning bar. When they've had enough for awhile, a private space under the platform offers retreat. Design: Playscapes.

Versatile sideyard structure

Built of hefty timbers, the climbing-swinging-karate structure shown below won't totter, even under a neighborhood onslaught.

Its three tall 8 by 8-inch pressure-treated Douglas fir posts (or substitute redwood) are set, 2 feet deep, in concrete cubes , shorter ones in 18-inch cubes. Beams are secured with countersunk bolts. Several lengths of galvanized pipe protrude from holes drilled through the posts; caps screwed on their threaded

ends safely finish them off to make climbing bars.

The long pair of cantilevered beams supports, interchangeably, a vertical tire swing or a karate bag. Either hooks onto a heavy eyebolt attached to a wide galvanized U that fits snugly between the beams.

Tops of the tallest posts are beveled and decorated with 2-inch-wide notches, and the entire structure is finished with a dark preservative. Redwood chips cushion the ground below it.

The structure was designed with versatility in mind, and each child in the family has a favorite use for it. Younger kids prefer climbing and swinging on the cantilevered tire. An older son needed to hang his karate bag where it could be kicked and chopped from all sides. And an older daughter favors gymnastic tricks on the galvanized-pipe bar linked between the central and furthermost posts. Landscape architects: Eriksson, Peters & Thoms.

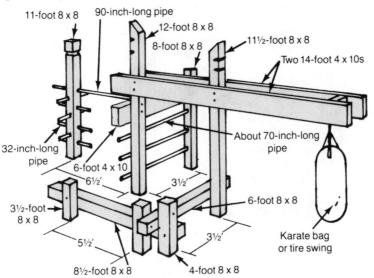

11-foot 8 x 8
90-inch-long pipe
12-foot 8 x 8
8-foot 8 x 8
11½-foot 8 x 8
Two 14-foot 4 x 10s
32-inch-long pipe
About 70-inch-long pipe
6-foot 4 x 10
6½'
3½'
3½-foot 8 x 8
6-foot 8 x 8
5½'
3½'
8½-foot 8 x 8
4-foot 8 x 8
Karate bag or tire swing

Ingredients for a first kiddie corral

A toddler's play space needn't be large—keep in mind that, like the sandbox or swing that occupies it, the play yard won't be used for more than a few years. But it should be generous enough to accommodate two or more kids happily.

For children younger than school age, the yard should be enclosed; it's also wise to carpet the ground with something soft, but kids need hard, smooth surfaces, too, for riding wheel toys. Keep in mind sun and shade patterns (you might want to plant a fast-growing tree in the play yard) and possible wind problems.

Keeping them off the street

Though it needn't be higher than about 3 feet, some sort of barricade is a must for keeping small children away from dangerous places, like busy streets.

The greatest security is provided by a metal fence of small chain links or welded wire, though these may look a bit barren without greenery. Some chain link fencing has spaces large enough for climbing, but wood slats inserted vertically will block off potential hand and foot holds. A fence of vertical boards is unclimbable by tots—but avoid splintery wood.

Play yard planning—For fun & practicality

Cushioning falls

Besides providing a good "drag strip" of smooth paving (for how-to details, consult the *Sunset* book *Walks, Walls & Patio Floors*), it's a good idea to provide the play area with a spongy ground cover—particularly where kids are most likely to take an occasional spill.

• Sand is undoubtedly the safest cushion for falls. And if you've ever taken a small girl or boy to the seashore, you know about the immediate appeal of sand, especially in vast expanses.

The more liberal the amount, the better. A depth of about 12 inches is not too much. Some public playgrounds feature "sand pools," scooped-out places with a thin layer of asphalt topped by 12 to 16 inches of sand. Each has several drainage holes filled with rock and topped with straw to keep sand out of them. (More details about sand appear on page 71.)

• Wood chips are a neater alter-native. One cubic yard will cover 100 square feet to a depth of about 3 inches, providing a fairly good buffer for children's falls in most situations (but increase the depth to 5 or 6 inches under a swing). To keep the chips from blowing about in the wind, you'll need to dampen them from time to time. Use coarsely ground fir bark if you can. Pine bark is more likely to cause splinters.

• Smooth gravel (1/2 to 3/4-inch pebbles) makes a practical cushioning surface. Gravel is less expensive than wood chips, dries quickly, and requires virtually no upkeep. A 3-ton load will cover an area of 150 square feet to a depth of 3 inches.

• Grass isn't quite as spongy a carpet as the materials listed above, but it still makes a good play surface. Most seed companies offer different mixtures of rugged, easy-to-grow varieties (but avoid mixtures that include clover, since it attracts bees). For maximum cushioning, keep the grass about 2 inches high.

A skateboard run

What sidewalk surfer wouldn't like a smooth, 4-foot-wide, concrete track complete with banked turns, sharp and gradual downhill drops, a small jump—and no cars in sight?

One grownup skateboarder built just such a track, with the help of his young nephews. First they contoured, soaked, and foot-packed a sandy slope; then they troweled concrete about 2 inches thick directly over the moist earth. The concrete was covered for a few days to help it cure without cracking (where soil is less stable, be sure to reinforce the concrete with wire mesh).

Children's play area

Hopscotch →

Garden

Pond

Bridge

A garden of children's delights

Rattle over a wooden plank bridge, skip down the hopscotch path shown at left, hop over the last square (if you hit it, a hidden doorbell will ring), and you're there —in the children's private play area. It doesn't look like much, but it has what makes kids happy: trees, dirt, water, secret hideaways, and room for imagination.

The play yard plan shown above started when one family had a flat back-of-the-house area bulldozed into irregular humps. Then they planted low-maintenance trees and shrubs to make a woodsy surrounding.

When the kids are feeling active, they can use standard play equipment set up in the center of the woods. On hot days they can soak their feet in a shallow 4 by 6-foot parent-built pond or in the stream into which the pond flows. Both are lined with plastic under pebbles, and edged with larger rocks. Perforations in the plastic allow some water to seep out, irrigating plants along the banks (leakage also prevents stagnation when the stream isn't running).

Guests beware: A valve hidden behind rocks adjusts a spray nozzle in the pond's center from dribble to geyser.

Swing seats & rigging

Tires and heavy inner tubes make good seats for either solitary or sociable swinging; some good tire ideas appear on pages 88 and 89. At toy shops you can find inexpensive plastic seats that cause no serious harm with an accidental thump. Or if you live near a boat supplier, try a boat fender (sketched above). Made of rubber and filled with either air or foam, it is 18 inches of lightweight length, with holes at either end for threading rope through.

Rope is probably a safer swing rigging than chain, simply because it is soft—but chains are good, too, and sometimes easier to link evenly to hardware. Use nylon rope for durability; cotton is just as strong, and easier on the hands when the swing doubles as a Tarzan-vine, but cotton is not weatherproof and will need more frequent replacement.

It isn't easy to find common hardware that will prevent friction from wearing through ropes or chains, in time. Metal nautical thimbles from a boat supplier ease friction. Or, if you rig a tire swing on a swivel or ball joint (used on the swing shown in the photograph opposite), friction will be lessened. And if you loop ropes or chains around a tree limb or fully accessible patio beam, encasing them in lengths of old garden hose will cut down on wear. See "Anchor it safely," page 57, for further safety tips.

With its lulling-to-thrilling motion, a garden swing is a true classic of childhood—one of the few pleasures that our kids can experience in exactly the same fashion as their grandparents once did.

If there appears to be no practical purpose to swinging, it's because there actually isn't much, save a little muscle-flexing once you learn to pump and a certain amount of mother-bossing ("Push me! Higher!") before you do. However, for both woolgathering and simple gladness, swings are unbeatable.

Slides, on the other hand, challenge you (if you're very small) to earn your breathless thrill. First you must come to terms with getting up them, then with an instant of terror before you dare to let go and swoop downward. This is why gentle, not-too-lofty slides (like the wide one shown opposite) may be the friendliest choice for young children.

For the very young, a wide slide

There are several advantages to a wide and not-too-high slide. Kids don't have to wait so long for their turns when two—or even three—can slip down together (besides, it's more sociable that way). And a generous width accommodates unusual antics more safely than do traditional playground types.

Construction details are given below for a simple 36-inch-wide plywood slide that bolts to the upright posts of a play platform.

If you face a slide toward the north, its metal surface will be less likely to become burning hot in the summer. Another trick is to use plastic laminate, in white or a pastel shade, instead of a metal surface. Just as slick, it won't heat up as much.

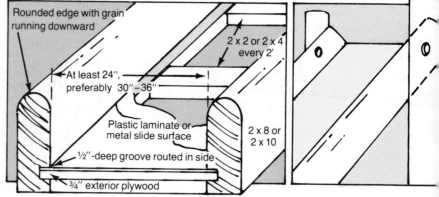

Rounded edge with grain running downward

At least 24", preferably 30"–36"

2 x 2 or 2 x 4 every 2'

Plastic laminate or metal slide surface

½"-deep groove routed in side

¾" exterior plywood

2 x 8 or 2 x 10

Slick but cool sliding surface is plastic laminate glued to plywood. (See drawing on facing page.) Design: Peter O. Whiteley.

Two, even three little kids can swing and twirl together on this swivel-mounted tire. Design: Peter O. Whiteley.

Thinking big...
Complex play rigs invite the neighbors in

The big, labyrinthine structures shown on these two pages can happily absorb a whole crowd of energetic kids at once. They offer enough variety that nobody ever gets bored—and there's ample scope for inventive games.

If you'd like to build a backyard structure on an ambitious scale, it will help to consult a playground designer—especially if you want to incorporate such hard-to-find materials as towering poles or a ship's cargo net.

Hefty beams jutting out from a two-story playhouse support a trapeze bar and swings— with room for extras later on. Design: Michael Moyer.

Visit schools, day-care centers, and parks where the outdoor equipment designs are exciting and versatile. Ask for references; parents and teachers may have done the building, but an architect who specializes in children's outdoor play is likely to have done the designing.

The softest surfacing underneath these structures is sand. Alternative materials and details on coverage are listed on page 80.

Navigating a cargo net is fun, because it wiggles beneath you. This one, slightly spread out, also makes a fine, roomy hammock.

Rocking and revolving tire swing is suspended from a swivel affixed to the beams of the structure shown also in the other two photographs on this page.

They zip down a sleek metal slide. Sand makes an agreeably soft landing pad. Design: Playscapes.

Balance, tone, stretch & strengthen... Ideas for junior gymnasts

Everyone in the family (maybe a few neighbors, as well) can enjoy backyard gymnastics with one of the easy-to-build exercise devices described here. You don't have to be Olympic material, necessarily—but if handstands or arm walking bring out the ham in you, all the better.

As you put this equipment together, keep safety in mind. Round all sharp edges and, to minimize splinters, sand the wood vigorously. Use the devices on level grassy ground, if you can.

To make them weather resistant, use resorcinal glue, and coat with a nonslippery exterior polyurethane or marine varnish.

A tumbling mat makes a soft landing pad for rolls, flips, and the occasional spill, yet it's also firm enough to give steady support when you traverse it on your hands.

It's hard work—but fun. Made of cotton, the rope won't hurt his hands; it's quite strong, but must be taken down in wet weather.

Less threatening than a fence top or tree limb, a balance beam offers the same off-the-ground experience. This unusual version also slopes gently from one end to the other. (Directions for a simpler balance beam appear on the facing page.) Design: Sam and Rita Eisenstat.

Low balance beam

Most of us more senior types had to grow up without the benefits to our physical and intellectual development of walking a balance beam. Some of us may have been lucky enough to "tightrope" walk a brick wall or sidewalk crack once in awhile, which amounts to almost the same thing.

At any rate, the balance beam (see drawing at right, and bottom photograph, opposite) has won much praise, over the last several decades, from educators who say that it bestows far-reaching benefits to small children who navigate it. Those benefits are said to range from gazelle-like grace to quicker absorption of reading skills. For older kids, the balance beam offers a place to do the splits or a handstand with a little more style than on ordinary lawn.

To make a simple balance beam, you glue and clamp together two 7-foot 2 by 4s (a single 4 x 4 would warp more easily). Cut notches 3-1/2 inches wide and 3 inches deep in both support blocks (8-inch-high 2 by 6s). Sand all edges smooth. Screw a metal joist hanger to the bottom of each notched block. Position and screw on bases of 2 by 6, as shown. To assemble, fit the two balance boards into the two supports (it should be a snug fit).

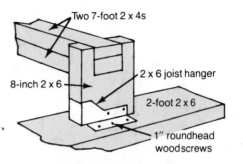

Two 7-foot 2 x 4s
8-inch 2 x 6
2 x 6 joist hanger
2-foot 2 x 6
1" roundhead wood screws

Handstand assists

These handy little wood grips, commonly used in gymnastics classes, further the pleasures of backbends, leg lifts, and hand or headstands.

Cut four trapezoid shapes from plywood; round top corners; drill 1-1/4-inch holes all the way through the top center of each. Apply glue inside holes and around ends of dowels; fit dowels in place. Sand thoroughly when dry.

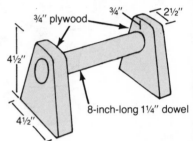

¾" plywood
¾"
2½"
4½"
4½"
8-inch-long 1¼" dowel

Shortened parallel bars

For arm walking, arm dips, leg lifts, leg swings— and other uses that kids will invent on their own— what your backyard may need is a set of these parallel bars.

Saw tapered tops on four 2 by 4-inch uprights, and drill holes 1-1/2 inches deep in their ends (as shown below) for dowel plugs. Cup the plywood base pieces and glue and nail or bolt these to the uprights. Drill an inch-deep hole 6-3/4 inches from the end of each banister rail; insert dowel plugs, then glue plugs in place in uprights. Sand all edges smooth; varnish to make weatherproof.

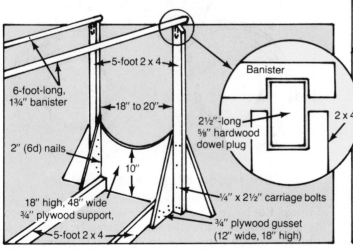

6-foot-long, 1¾" banister
5-foot 2 x 4
18" to 20"
Banister
2½"-long ⅝" hardwood dowel plug
2 x 4
2" (6d) nails
10"
18" high, 48" wide ¾" plywood support,
5-foot 2 x 4
¼" x 2½" carriage bolts
¾" plywood gusset (12" wide, 18" high)

The swingseat shown at left hangs from the steel-reinforced inner rings of a tire that has been turned inside out. Don't try to make it from a steel-belted tire— it's just about impossible to cut.

After scrubbing the tire, you slash it next to the inner ring, using a hacksaw. Cut away three-quarters of the tire's circumference.

Next, step on the tread and pull up hard on the rings to pop the tire inside out.

Rubbery tricks with tires & tubes

Easy to find and inexpensive

Toys made from tires have been hanging around backyards for generations. And for good reason: used tires are low in price or even free; they're easy to nail, bolt, or cut; and they're bouncy, soft, and virtually indestructible.

Finding old tires should be no problem. Service stations or tire shops are usually happy to donate a few rubber carcasses, especially those worn beyond the point of possible retreading. The same is true for inner tubes.

The first thing old tires usually need is a good scrub to wash away grime and black rubber dust. Then, to make most of the toys shown here—you need only a few easy-to-find supplies—rope, lag screws, and nuts and bolts (including U-bolts).

Six-tire totem pole for climbing

Six old tires and a pine pole make a durable vertical maze. Each tire is bolted to the pole with two 6-inch lag screws; they pass through a 2 by 4 by 8-inch block of wood inside the tire. Design: Ray Daykins.

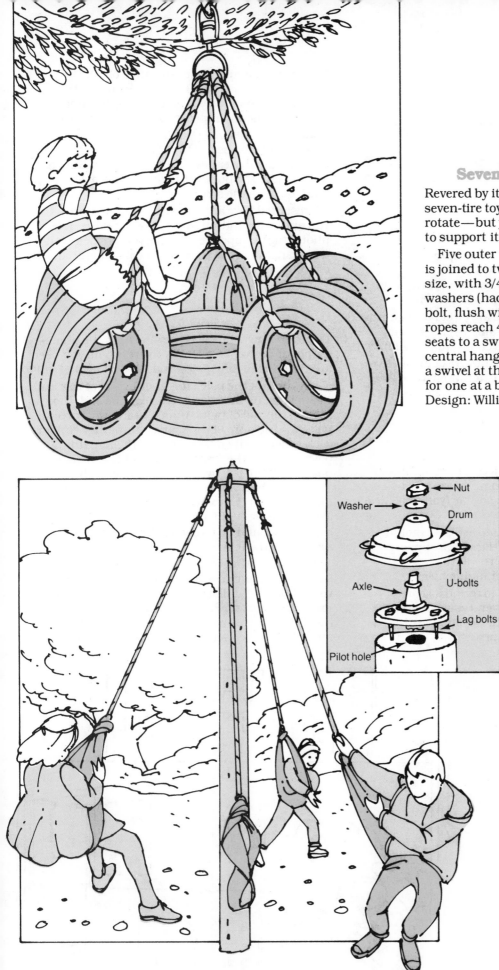

Seven-tire super swing

Revered by its young riders, this seven-tire toy can swing, rock, and rotate—but you'll need a big tree to support it.

Five outer tires form seats, and each is joined to two inner tires of the same size, with 3/4-inch bolts, nuts, and washers (hacksaw off the end of each bolt, flush with the nut). One-inch ropes reach 45 inches from the tire seats to a swivel joint attached to a central hanging rope. If you can't find a swivel at the hardware store, look for one at a boat supply store. Design: William Potts.

Nut

Washer

Drum

Axle

U-bolts

Lag bolts

Pilot hole

A swing-around of tubes

Instead of tires (which would be too heavy for the ride), deflated inner tubes carry the passengers who ride this wonderful merry-go-round.

The tubes hang by ropes from an auto wheel assembly, bought at an auto wrecking yard. Its sturdy ball bearings allow the swing-around to rotate. The detail at left shows how the wheel assembly goes together.

The swing-around's 16-foot pole was set 4 feet deep in concrete.

Little domiciles, forts & retreats

If we remember that—to small children—many rooms must look and even feel like cavernous spaces, then it's easy to understand the instant appeal of a cozy little playhouse.

Most kids, at some point, invent their own shelters, which may be as simple and temporary as sheets draped over lawn furniture. Certainly they'll want to join the building activities, even when an adult designs the structure.

Presented here are two miniature dwellings that you and your chidren might like to set up. The photographs opposite will give you an idea of the wide range of styles possible in this Lilliputian field of architecture.

Versatile box house

Designed as an architectural course project, this simple playhouse consists of two plywood boxes, one of them small enough that even a young child can move it to various sides of its larger mate.

Increasing its play potential are circular openings to crawl through, a movable ramp to creep up or slide down, and notches and a chain ladder to climb.

Sheathing pieces for both units are cut from two 4 by 8-foot sheets of 5/8-inch exterior plywood (see cutting diagram below, right).

The big unit, which is 5 feet long, 4 feet high and 2 feet wide, has a frame of standard 2 by 2-inch lumber. Its 2-foot-square companion is built of 1 by 1-inch framing.

After cutting the plywood pieces, preassemble all the parts shown in the drawings (below, left) before gluing and nailing them to the frame (you may have to do some trimming).

The sides of the plywood ramp are base molding; plastic laminate makes its surface both slippery and splinter-free. A 1 by 1-inch lip at the top of the ramp locks inside any of the climbing holes.

After construction, be sure to round all corners and sand well. Finish with several coats of exterior paint or polyurethane varnish. Design: Cynthia Richardson and Merrilinn Zeppa.

Vegetable tepee

The framework for the tepee shown in the photograph, opposite, is very easy to erect —all you need are eight to ten long poles and a ball of heavy twine.

Lay three of the poles together in a neat row and, with twine, tie them securely near one end. Next, leaving the ball of twine uncut, stand the three poles up and spread them apart until they support each other —tripod fashion. Lay the remaining poles between the first three, spacing as equally as possible. Wrap the twine several times tightly around each as you lay it in place. When all are tied together, knot the twine and cut it from the ball, allowing at least 36 inches of extra length. Pull this length taut, and tie it toward the base of one pole, to help brace the tepee.

If you do all that in the spring, after danger of frost is past, and in a sunny corner of the garden, your child might like to raise some leafy coverage for the tepee base. Fast-growing and hardy, Kentucky Wonder beans (which can be harvested later for dinner) or scarlet runners make good tepee vines.

Charming little play cottage arrived as a hand-me-down from its site in an older friend's yard, then was painted to match the big house.

Scarlet runner beans—easy and quick to grow—drape Chelsea's beanpole tepee; its floor is carpeted with sand. See facing page for details.

Red, white, and blue graphic cube house makes a splashy addition to the backyard landscape.

This school has an everybody-built-it playground

Look what can happen to an elementary school when parents, kids, and teachers team up with an architect to build the playground of their dreams. It took quite a few hardworking weekends, but when it was finished, everybody from kindergarteners to sixth graders (not to mention their elders) felt a glow of proud accomplishment.

Equipment choices were based on the kids' own suggestions. Funds were collected partly through their efforts in such imaginative projects as a "sundae social" and a silent auction of such services as babysitting, dog walking, and tutoring younger children.

Everybody banded together in small groups to put up the equipment, each major chunk assigned to a team. Each team included one or two experts who taught their skills to the less experienced. It all began as a project of a parent-teacher organization. Architect: Hugh Kennedy.

Spooky to crawl through and great for chase games is this tunnel of welded steel barrels.

A quick slip down the slide rewards them after the joys of an arduous journey up, down, across, under, over, and through.

Free-wheeling monkey bars are hoops threaded on pipe; parallel bars in the background are chain encased in rubber hose.

Chain-linked tires knit together a swinging bridge that jiggles and jumps as kids work their way across.

Beyond the backyard... Playful & practical ideas for the whole family

We close this book with an eclectic assortment of outdoor ideas for the hale and hearty of virtually any age. Your kids can build the bike rack themselves, but chances are your own bike will be among the beneficiaries. And the ice-skating rink may inspire a wintry picnic party for the whole family, plus friends and neighbors.

The ideas shown in the photographs below offer not only playful appeal, but esthetic appeal as well. Basketball bouncing requires pavement, but pavement needn't look drab. Wading, instead of just walking, across a stone terrace is delicious fun—and the water refreshes the eye.

Soft colors painted on concrete glamorize a previously barren expanse. They also clarify zones for the players—the key, the free-throw line, and concentric lanes for games of Horse or Clock. Design: Art Ishida.

Cascading water spills down steps and into a wide, shallow pool—irresistible to barefoot kids, refreshing to their elders as well. Recirculated by a pump, the miniature water-falls splash alongside railroad tie steps that lead from street level to an entry deck below. Landscape architects: Michael Painter and Associates.

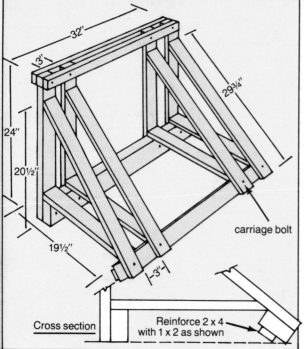

Cross section

32"

3"

24"

29¾"

20½"

19½"

3"

carriage bolt

Reinforce 2 x 4
with 1 x 2 as shown

Bike rack kids can build

The simple rack shown above is
sturdy and portable, and has been
tested by young carpenters in a Cub
Scout troup. Made of 1 by 2s and 2 by
4s, it can be lengthened to hold three
bikes if you increase its 32-inch di-
mension to 54 inches. But for more
than three bikes, you'd best make a
second rack.

Assemble the rack with twelve
1/4-inch-diameter carriage bolts
and washers placed as indicated in
the drawing; the other members
are simply nailed in place.

Icy idea from Alaska

Three families from the freezing North have
pioneered a simple way to make a skating rink from
fresh snow.

They trample smooth the first snow to form a
base rather like a gigantic pie shell. They then spray
the "shell" with water to form a glaze, repeating
gradually until the ice buildup is 2 to 3 inches thick.
Once the ice gets this thick, it's only a matter of
keeping snow and frost scraped off and smoothing
the rink by adding more water. In very cold weather,
when cracks appear, they simply fill them with
slush, smoothing the seams with a mason's trowel.

One family put a base of polyethylene sheeting
over the trampled snow; this method requires less
water for good ice buildup, but prolonged use could
damage grass underneath.

Beautiful basketball

Often the garage is the most practical place to
mount a basketball net. Often, too, the results are
somewhat unsightly. But with a little imaginative
planning, home basketball can be as esthetic as it is
athletic—note the graphic court shown on the facing page. Special paint for concrete is available in a
variety of colors at most paint stores.

Another family painted a graphic decoration on
the backboard itself. Going one step further, they
flood the backboard (which has perforations in its
design) with light at night, so that it also serves
to illuminate the parking area. The backboard
is a 58-inch disk made from two thicknesses of
3/4-inch plywood. Eight 1/2-inch-wide slits cut into
the disk glow when the floodlight goes on. A 2 by 4's
width behind the disk (see above) is an arc of the
same plywood (one thickness only, 4 feet high by 7
feet wide) with an 18-inch-diameter hole cut in its
center.

Bright yellow and orange against white, painted
with sign-painter's enamels, turn the disk into a
bold sunburst. Rainbow stripes decorate the arc.
Architect: David Wright.

Index